LOK KALYAN MARG

POLITICAL JOURNEY OF DEVELOPING INDIA

ARYAN J. PATIL

Made with ❤ on the Notion Press Platform
www.notionpress.com

Dedicated in the lotus feet of Mata Sita and
Prabhu Shree Ram

प्रणम्य शिरसा विष्णुं त्रैलोक्याधिपतिं प्रभुम् ।
भारतस्य राजनैतिकयात्रायाः विषये लेखनं आरभन्ते।

Contents

Foreword

The book "Lok Kalyan Marg" written by Aryan patil is very good and informative. Every important incident is covered in this book. A person who doesn't know politics at all would be knowing about this. Also, this first book is written by him which is very inspiring for others who just think about writing and never try. I liked the book a lot and I am sure everyone would like it. I recommend everyone to read it at least once. Trust me you will never regret it.
-Saurabh K. Surti

Preface

I

Aryan Patil

Welcome, all the reader friends who decided to read this book by giving their valuable time.

Lok Kalyan Marg describes the political journey of the World's largest democracy i.e. India. This book contains the journey from Jawaharlal Nehru to Narendra Modi. Information from various sources is collected, simplified and presented here. All the major events of Indian politics are covered in this book and tried to present in an elementary form. The language of this book is kept very simple so that readers of all age groups can understand. Aristotle once said that the study of Political Science is "the master of all sciences". The study of political science is very important in the everyday lives of the billions of people that live in the world today. The purpose of this book is to provide political knowledge to all readers. This is the first edition of this book and in future, I will try to make the book better than now. In future, new content will also be added to this book and with deep research, I will try to explain the current topics in more detail. I will do my best to put forth the content with complete honesty.

Readers are requested to give their valuable suggestions on Google Forms (Please scan the QR Code) to make this book better than now. I hope that you love this book.

Thank You.

❦❦❦

Acknowledgements

ԸԸԸ

Jitendra K. Patil
Sunita J. Patil
Dhruv J Maheshwari - Proof Reading and drafting
Saurabh K Surti - Proof Reading, drafting
Rajendra N. Patil - Book Cover Designer
(Narayan Printers and Graphic Designing)
Notion Press Publications - Book Publishing platform

ԸԸԸ

ONE
THE NEHRU ERA (1952-1964*)

""Facts are facts and will not disappear on account of your likes.""

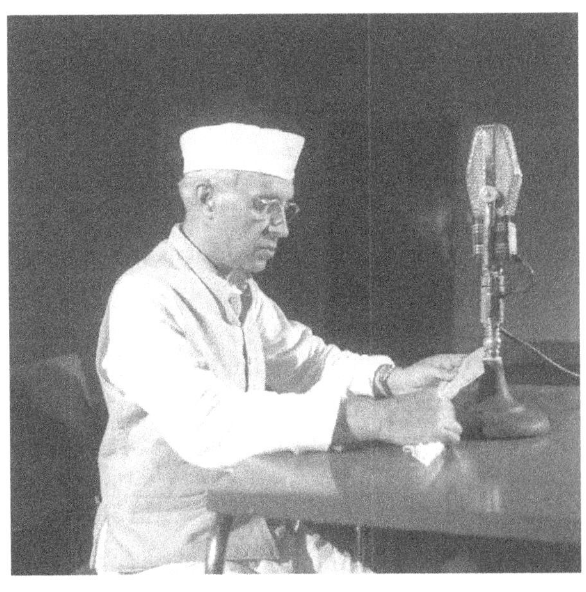

Jawaharlal Nehru

As a newly independent country, there were lots of challenges. Handling such a vast country with a population of 340 million people (approx.) was not easy; the wounds of the partition of the country and the pain of losing loved ones cannot be described in words. On **26ᵗʰ November 1949**, the constitution was ready and on **26ᵗʰ January 1950**, the body was implemented. After the implementation of the Constitution Of India, under its provisions, India's 1ˢᵗ general elections were held between **25 October 1951 and 21 February 1952**. This was the first election to the Lok Sabha after independence. A total of **489 seats** were there which 53 parties and 533 independents contested. The supremacy of the Indian National Congress was at its peak. To challenge their supremacy, **Dr B.R Ambedkar** established **Scheduled Caste Federation** (which today is known as **Republican Party**) and **Syama Prasad Mukherjee** established **Jana Sangh** (which is today known as **Bharatiya Janta Party**). The results of the first general elections were not at all surprising as the INC maintained its superiority and won **364/489 seats.** Though the voter turnout was 45.7%, this election was the first step toward a democratic India. The Lok Sabha lasted its full term from 1**7 April 1952 until 4 April 1957.**

Jawaharlal Nehru became the 1ˢᵗ Prime Minister Of India. Now, let's talk about the first term of Nehru. Almost all the states were merged into the Union Of India till the 1950s (ex. Goa and Sikkim). Nehru stressed the concept of **Pan-Indianism** and refused to divide states based on religion and ethnicity. Pan-Indianism is just a political theory of promoting unity (in simple words). Nehru appointed the **States Reorganisation Commission(SRC)** in **December 1953** to prepare for the creation of states on linguistic lines. This commission was headed by **Justice Fazal Ali** and so it is also known as **Fazal Ali Commission.** The reports were submitted in 1956 by **Justice Fazal Ali, K.M. Panikkar and H.N Kunzru.** SRC suggested (1) the three-tier (Part A/B/C) states should be abolished, (2) The institution of Rajapramukh and special agreement with former princely states should be abolished (3) The general control vested in the Government of India by Article 371 should be abolished (4) Only the following 3 states should be the Union Territories: Andaman & Nicobar, Delhi and Manipur. The other part-C/D territories should be merged with the adjoining states. Part II of Report of the States Reorganisation Commission (SRC) 1955, titled "Factors Bearing on Reorganisation", the Commission clearly said that "it is neither possible nor desirable to reorganise States based on the single test of either language or culture, but that a balanced approach to the whole problem is necessary for the interest of our national unity." SRC was implemented in 1955, though there were controversies also.

Nehru's popularity was increasing day by day. In 1955, Churchill called Nehru, the light of Asia, and a **greater light than Gautama Buddha**. Nehru is considered the creator of the Modern Indian State. After the exit of Subhash Chandra Bose from Indian politics and the death of Sardar Patel, Nehru was the only superior leader who remained in India. So obviously, he faced no hindrance in his work. Now, Nehru can implement his basic policies easily. Nehru implemented several economic policies and especially he stressed replacing imports with domestic production (ISI i.e. Import Substitution Industrialisation) and also introduced India to the concept of a **Mixed Economy**. He believed the establishment of basic and heavy industry was fundamental to the development and modernisation of the Indian economy. The government, therefore, directed investment primarily into key public sector industries—steel, iron, coal, and power—promoting their development with subsidies and protectionist policies. Nehru introduced the policy of **Non-Alignment** due to which India got financial and technical support from both power blocks which helped to develop India's industrial base. Interestingly, India's GDP was around 4% and America's GDP was 8.0% in the 1950s. Successful land reform was introduced that abolished giant landholdings, but efforts to redistribute land by limiting landownership failed.

Nehru also put forth the concept of National Universities like the **All India Institute Of Medical Sciences** (AIIMS), **Indian Institute Of Technology** (IIT), **Indian Institute Of Management** (IIM), and the **National Institute Of Technology** (NIT). He also committed to guaranteeing free and compulsory primary education to all of India's children and also fought against malnutrition. Nehru also added the reservation systems to eradicate the inequalities faced by Scheduled Caste people. He also enacted many changes to Hindu law to criminalise caste discrimination and increase the legal rights and social freedoms of women. Nehru enacted the Official Languages Act in 1963 to ensure the continuing use of English beyond 1965. Nehru was the only man who started nuclear studies in India. He appointed **Homi J Bhabha** and gave him complete nuclear-related authority and told him to only report to the Prime Minister. (Complete story discussed in Chapter 11)

It's time for the 1957 General Elections. This time too, all the parties were not strong enough to break the supremacy of the Indian National Congress, which secured 371 out of 494 seats. **Praja Socialist Party** (PSP) was born when **Archarya Kriplani's Kisan Majdoor Praja Party (KMPP)** and **Jayaprakash Narayan's Socialist Party** merged, securing 19 seats, a clear loss of 2 seats, **Communist Party Of India** (CPI) managed to increase their seats by 11. 1962 General Election results indicated that people's faith in the Communist Parties increased. Also, right-wing political parties like **Akhil Bharatiya Jana Sangh (ABJS)** (today's BJP) succeeded in making their way into mainstream politics. Though Nehru managed to lead congress towards victory. This indicated that the congress party is losing its supremacy.

Today he is criticized for many of his decisions. Nehru being Prime Minister is today itself a controversy. **Sardar Patel** was the official choice of the then Congress Party but Gandhiji focused on Nehru's choice. After 1950, the post-Patel-Gandhi Era, Nehru was the only supreme and decision-making authority of Congress and due to his behaviour, many of his colleagues left the cabinet. Nehru conducted India's foreign policy singlehanded, giving it a direction that he thought was right. Nehru's half-hearted application of socialism produced a hugely chaotic situation, the burden of the country carried for over half a century. Moreover, Nehru believed in non-violence and he believed that India needed no army as we have no enemies. In spite being failure to learn from the past. Pakistan's attack on Kashmir in 1948 gave birth to POK, and his blindfolded trust in the Kashmiri leadership lead to Article 370. His blindfolded trust in the communist ideologies of China resulted in the **1962 Sino-Indian War**, which gave birth to **Aksai Chin.** These are not mistakes, these are blunders, that too being a barrister. During Nehru's rule, many conflicts took place between Congress Party and the then Government. Due to these conflicts, Acharya Kriplani resigned from his position in the Congress party. Though, today also, Nehru is praised for his blunders by some of the so-called **"intellectuals"**. They all are right on their way.

TWO

MAN OF PEACE - SHRI. LAL BAHADUR SHASTRI (1964-1966*)

"I am not as simple as I look."

Shastriji with Kamaraj and Nehru

Nehru's health steadily started declining in 1962. Some intellectuals believed that this was due to the Sino-Indian War and the betrayal of China. On 27 May 1964, Nehru died due to a **heart attack.** This was a turning point in Indian politics. There was no one to replace Nehru! This was the end of the Nehru Era. Now the biggest question raised is, "Who after Nehru?" **Gulzarilal Nanda** was declared the interim Prime Minister Of India to maintain the stability of the country, but the question was as it is! At this point, India needed a leader who would continue to carry forward Nehru's legacy, especially at the time when the Congress party was losing its supremacy. This time, **Morarji Desai** was a strong competitor. **K. Kamaraj** (also famous for the **Kamaraj Plan**), the then president of the Congress Party, wanted Lal Bahadur Shastri to be the successor of Jawaharlal Nehru. On **9 June 1964**, **Lal Bahadur Shastri** was sworn in as the 2nd Prime Minister of Independent India. Shastri Ji was a soft-spoken man and he retained many members of Nehru's Cabinet. Gulzarilal Nanda as Home Minister, **T.T Krishnamacharya** as Finance Minister, **Yashvantrao Chauhan** as Defence Minister, and **Indira Gandhi** became Information and Broadcasting Minister.

Shastriji continued Nehru's legacy and ideologies as this can be noticed in many of his key decisions. Too many challenges were there, and there was a lot to improve. India was dependent on foreign countries for daily commodities like Wheat, Rice, etc. to a great extinct. Demand was increasing but the production was steady and so, India was facing a chronic food shortage across the country. The biggest challenge in front of Shastriji was to make India a self-sufficient country. He promoted **White Revolution** by setting up **National Dairy Development Board (NDDB)** and supported **Anand Milk Union Limited (AMUL)**. This resulted in tremendous milk production in the country and soon India became the largest milk producer in the World. This is all possible due to the joint efforts and visionary ideas of **Dr Verghese Kurien** and Shastriji. He also promoted **Green Revolution** in the country. He requested people to skip a meal a week and soon he got a great response across the country. Before requesting, he started the same from his home. He motivated people across the country to maximise the production of food grains. He started farming at his official residence in New Delhi.

Shastriji gave a fantastic slogan in the **Urwa** village of **Allahabad**, "Jay Jawan, Jay Kisan" at the time of the **Indo-Pakistan war** in 1965. India faced Indo-Pakistan War for the 2nd time in 1965. Pakistani Army crossed the **Line Of Control (LOC)** disguised as Kashmiri locals and tried to capture **Akhnoor** in Jammu as a part of **"Operation Grand Slam"**. India threatened Pakistan by crossing the International border near **Lahore** and told them to pull its forces back. The War lasts for **22 days** and finally, the results were in favour of India. Both countries agreed to a ceasefire and finally, **Tashkent Declaration** was signed in **USSR** (today's **Uzbekistan**). This treaty was criticized by both countries as both were expecting more than they got. Also, this event, later on, proved to be the most shocking event for the entire country and an unexpected turn in Indian Politics. Yes, Shastriji was now no more.......

On 11th January 1966, Early in the morning, it was officially declared this news through Aakashwani. It was declared that the death was due to cardiac arrest, but there was no post-mortem conducted by USSR! Shastriji's family deny agreeing to it. Shastriji's death is considered as India's one of the biggest mysteries of Indian Politics. It is debated a lot of times in this country. It has also been raised as a political issue. Many documentaries and films have been shot on this topic. This issue continued to be used only for public attention and for political gains, till now this remained a mystery. **Gulzarilal Nanda** again assumed the office of interim Prime Minister Of India till further decision and this topic ended up being a mystery.

I want to share some interesting facts about Shastri ji. It is well known that Shastri was imprisoned many times during his freedom struggle. However, his political commentator Dr Sandeep Shastri clarifies in his book Lal Bahadur Shastri: Politics and Beyond (2019) revealed that his daughter Suman became seriously ill during that time. Shastri was given her 15-day probation period, but sadly his daughter passed away within that time limit. With sheer courage, he quickly returned to spend his time.

In another case, he discovered in prison that his wife was able to save 10 rupees from a 50 rupee pension paid by a civil society servant. Considering the income to be superfluous, he asked the organization set up by Lala Lajpat Rai to cut his pension and donate the 10 rupees he had saved to those in need.

Shastriji was a simple man but India lost this diamond too early.

❧❧❧

THREE

IRON LADY - SMT. INDIRA GANDHI (1966-1977)

"The power to question is the basis of all human progress."

Indira Gandhi with U.S. President George Bush

A political race started in India before the mortal remains of Shastriji reached Delhi. Many leaders started making solid claims about the Prime Minister's post. Once again, the same question arose after 18 months in front of **K. Kamaraj, "Who will be the next?"** This time, **Gulzarilal Nanda, Morarji Desai, and Indira Gandhi** were three strong names in front of K. Kamaraj. Kamaraj wanted to solve this matter internally without any elections and the unanimous consent of the Congress Party. Because Morarji Desai's position was super solid and many intellectuals believed it was impossible to beat him in party elections. But **K. Kamaraj** put forth the name of **Indira Gandhi** asPrime Minister, but Morarji Desai wanted parliament elections, and the result was in favour of Indira Gandhi. On **January 19, 1996**, Indira Gandhi was sworn in as the 3rd Prime Minister of India and Morarji Desai was sworn in as Deputy Prime Minister of India. The main reason why Indira Gandhi was elected was that she was the daughter of Jawaharlal Nehru. The second reason can be understood further. During the 1st year of her office, it can be noticed that she lacked confidence, and that's why she was widely criticized by the media and opposition and was named a **"Goongy Gudia"** as she was used as a tool by the **Syndicate Group** of the Congress Party. A syndicate is a group of non-Hindi-speaking high-profile leaders of the Indian National Congress who wield significant power and influence within the party.

Here come the **1967 General Elections**. This was the first election without Nehru. This time, the **Swatantra Party (SWA)**, led by **C. Rajgopalachari**, and the **Akhil Bharatiya Jan Sangh (ABJS)**, led by **Pt. Deendayal Upadhyay**, got strong, and the influence of the right-wing party increased in India. As a result, ABJS won 35 seats and became the 3rd largest party in India, while **SWA** won **44 seats** and became the 2nd largest party in India. The Communist Party lost its vote bank compared to the 1962 general elections. Due to ideological differences between some groups in CPI, they got separated and set up a new party named the **Communist Party of India (Marxist).** Congress won only 283 seats, 78 fewer than in the 1962 General Elections. This was the lowest tally of seats in Congress till now. Nealy half of the ministers of Indira's cabinet lost their seats. This was also seen at the state level. Congress lost power from 9 states-Madhya Pradesh, Kerala, Madras, Uttar Pradesh, Punjab, Haryana, Bihar, West Bengal, and Odisha. By 1967, India's annual economic growth was only 2%, which was due to the **1962 Sino-Indian War** and the **1965 Indo-Pakistan War.** When Lal Bahadur Shastri was Prime Minister of India, the government's popularity increased, but after his death, clashes started between Indira Gandhi and Morarji Desai, the then Prime Minister and Deputy Prime Minister of India respectively. So on **4 March 1967**, Indira Gandhi swore again as the Prime Minister of India and **Morarji Desai** as **Deputy Prime Minister of India**.

The first tenure of Indira Gandhi began in 1967 with several challenges. For the first time, the congress party lost the majority of states. The main challenge for Indira was not the opposition, it was her party, **"The Syndicates"**. Syndicates want Indira to work as per them but Indira silently cornered them aside and she trusted to go with some of her trusted advisors. Internal clashes between the congress party and Indira Gandhi increased on many issues like the Presidential candidate of 1969, where she supported independent candidate **V.V. Gir**i despite supporting **Neelam Sanjiv Reddy** (official Presidential candidate of the Congress Party), 2- the Nationalisation of Banks without consulting the Finance Minister, 3- Devaluation of Rupee which created a mess for Indian businessman and traders, socialist policies, etc. **S. Nijalingappa** expelled her from the party and this was the time for the splitting of the congress party. Finally, Congress Party split into two groups as Indira Gandhi separated and gave shape to her own Congress named Indian National **Congress (Requisitionists) (INC-R)**. Moreover, she retained 218 MPs (nearly) on her side. INC-R lost the majority in parliament but remained in power with the help of some of the regional parties like **DMK** and **CPI**. This was India's first minority government. This scenario gave birth to a new concept in Indian Politics and that was the **"Coalition Government Theory"** as there was no clear majority for any of the political parties. **Samyukta Vidhayak Dal (SVD)** was a coalition of parties formed by the **Bharatiya Kranti Dal, the Samyukta Socialist Party, the Praja Socialist Party, and the Jana Sangh**. This was formed to fight against the Congress Party. In 1967, when Congress was losing state assembly elections, the majority of them were replaced by SVD. V.V. Giri was sworn in as the President of India on **24 August 1969**. He was the only independent candidate to win the Presidential Elections. He unopposedly used to accept all the decisions of Madam Prime Minister. He was a very loyal personality to Madam Prime Minister. He was not the President Of India, he was the "personal president of Madam", a complete and pure "rubberstamp" of the Prime Minister of India. Giri unquestioningly accepted Indira Gandhi's decision to sack the **Charan Singh** ministry in Uttar Pradesh and advised her to go in for early elections in 1971. Time passed in all this political drama till 1971 when early elections took place in India.

The 1971 Indian General Elections were the 5th Loksabha elections of India which were going to decide the fate of Indira Gandhi. The 27 Indian states and territories represented 518 seats of the lower house. Two slogans became famous this year 1- **"Garibi Hatao"**, and 2- **"Indira Hatao"**. **"Garibi Hatao"** gained tremendous momentum and targeted both- the rural as well as the urban public. Also, the intention behind this slogan was to sweep from caste-based politics quietly and to get a clear resounding majority. The program was supervised and staffed by the Indian National Congress party. "These programs also provided the central political leadership with new and vast patronage resources to be disbursed throughout the country." Indira Gandhi won a resounding victory in this election by winning 352 seats and emerged as the single largest party. CPI(M) emerged as the 2nd largest party followed by CPI-DMK in 3rd and ABJS as 4th. Kamaraj's Congress was finished, left with only 16 seats in the complete Lok Sabha.

On **15 March 1971**, Indira Gandhi swore in again as the Prime Minister Of India. This was the biggest achievement of Indira Gandhi. The second most was the **Bangladesh Liberation War.** On **3rd December 1971**, Indira Gandhi officially announced on **All India Radio** that the Pakistan fighters attacked **Amritsar, Pathankot, Srinagar, Awantipura, Uttarlai, Jodhpur, Ambala, and Agra Airbases.** Earlier, Indira promised to free East Pakistan from the chains of Pakistan and also promised to help the **Bangladesh Muktivahini.** So she ordered the Army to head towards Dhaka and the Air force started throwing bombs on West Pakistan airbases. Pakistan planned to capture from the Western side i.e. Jaisalmer, Ramgarh, Longewala, and Barmer under the leadership of **Pakistani Brigadier Tariq M. Mir.** Only 83 Indian soldiers were on duty at the Longewala post that night. Indian troops handled and fought the Pakistani troops under the leadership of **Major Kuldip Singh Changpuri, 23 Punjab Regiment** that night finally in the morning, the Indian Airforce took countermeasures under **"Operation Trident".** On **5 December 1971**, Indian Navvy destroyed the **Karachi Harbour, Cox Bazar, and Chittagong.** This was only possible because of India's only aircraft carrier ship, **INS Vikrant.** Indian Navy destroyed **PNS Ghazi** carrying 93 soldiers near **Vishakhapatnam** with the help of **INS Rajput.** Indira Gandhi declared in parliament the recognition of Bangladesh on **6th December 1971.** The only motto behind this was to slap America who was helping Pakistan from the backside and even raised this issue in **United Nations Security Council (UNSC).** Still, he failed to do so as Russia used its veto power in favour of India. Due to the **Indian-Soviet Treaty Of Friendship and Co-operation** signed in 1971, Russia completely supported India, despite international pressure. On **14 December 1971**, India attacked the residence of the Governor General of East Pakistan along with **Mukti Vahini.** Just the previous day, Niazi has famously declared in front of a camera to Associated Press newsmen, **"We will fight to the last."** And the very next day, General Niazi wrote a letter of surrender to India. On 16th December 1971, at Dhaka Race Course Road, **A.A.K Niazi** officially surrendered to India by signing the Instrument of Surrender on behalf of the Pakistan Eastern command. At 17:30 hours IST, Indira Gandhi officially declared that **"Dhaka is now a free capital of a free country"**. The Instrument Of Surrender was signed in Dhaka at 16:31 hours IST by Lt. Gen. AAK Niazi on behalf of Pakistan Eastern Command. **Lt. Gen. Jagjit Singh Arora** GOC-in-Command of the Indian and Bangladesh forces in the Eastern Theatre accepted the surrender." Post-victory, Indira Gandhi was quick to announce a ceasefire. She made it clear to the world that India's ambitions were not territorial nor was it revengeful or expansionist. Throughout 1971, she gave the maximum weightage and importance to military commanders and did not act in panic or impulse. Atal Bihari Vajpayee, then one of the front-ranking Opposition leaders, described Indira Gandhi as **'Abhinav Chandi Durga'** for defeating Pakistan in the war. Vajpayee's description of Indira Gandhi as Durga helped the Congress leader cultivate a larger-than-life image.

Both the countries settled down and now it was time for the Peace Treaty. Several conferences took place in Shimla. The treaty's official purpose was stated to serve as a way for both countries to **"put an end to the conflict and confrontation that have hitherto marred their relations"** and to conceive the steps to be taken for further normalization of India–Pakistan relations while also laying down the principles that should govern their future interactions. The draft of this treaty proposed was laid 6 times on the table and finally, On 3rd July 1972 at 12:40 Hrs IST, The treaty assigned by **Zulfikar Ali Bhutto** and Indira Gandhi at Shimla and hence, it was known as **"The Shimla Agreement"**. Pakistan wanted third-party involvement in this matter but Indira Gandhi strongly refused to do so. India promised to return the captured land to Pakistan and also the soldiers under Indian custody. In return, Pakistan agreed to solve all the other matters through bilateral conversations. Till now, nothing solved between both nations and I don't think it is possible in the future at least till the next 10-15 years. Both leaders kept their silence on the Kashmir issue and the only reason was their political supremacy in their countries. Despite winning the war in 1971, India failed in Shimla Agreement. Pakistan broke the ceasefire several times.

On May 18, 1974, India conducted her first nuclear test successfully at **Pokhran** in Rajasthan. With this, India became the world's sixth nuclear power outside the five permanent members of the United Nations. India characterised the test as a peaceful nuclear explosion. The US took offence to this, blocked aid to India and imposed numerous sanctions. The issue caused a stalemate in the relations between the two countries. However, the United States made amends when she realised that the test did not violate any agreement, and sent a shipment of enriched uranium for the **Tarapur Reactor**, making the rest of the world accept the status of India as a responsible nuclear power. The relationship between India and the Soviet Union deepened during Indira Gandhi's rule. The support of the Soviets with arms supplies, and the use of the veto at the United Nations, helped India in winning and consolidating its victory over Pakistan in the 1971 Bangladesh liberation war. Subsequently, the Soviet Union became the main arms supplier during the rule of Indira Gandhi.

Indira became a political personality and her fame increased in India as well as Bangladesh after the 1971 Bangladesh Liberation War. Even opposition leaders started praising Indira for her work. Soon, Indira's Congress Party won a series of state assembly elections in India and Congress regain its supremacy in India. She became an icon for the poor and underprivileged people and also an influential national leader. All the state assembly elections were fought in Indira's face. **"Indira Wave"** captured the whole country except Tamil Nadu and thus gained fame but the complete dependency was on the popularity of the supreme leader i.e. Indira Gandhi. It was like, "कांग्रेस को बचाने के चक्कर में पूरे कांग्रेस को ही बदल डाला". Besides the 1971 War, Indira Gandhi faced a lot of challenges like the 1973 Oil Crisis, External emergency, War expenses, Drought situations, high inflation, Unemployment, low Industrial development, food crisis, etc. Indira Gandhi wanted the complete system to work according to her and at her fingertips. She captured almost the whole system, even the president but the judiciary was independent! She wanted a "committed judiciary" in India- in simple language, a judiciary that gives all the decisions in favour of the central government and creates no hurdle in government work. Indira wanted to change the fundamentals of the Indian Constitution and even she tried to do so by bringing the 24th and 25th Amendments of the Indian Constitution on 5th November 1971 stating that the parliament has the complete right to amend any part of the constitution even the fundamentals of the Indian Constitution! Supreme Court In 1967's **Golaknath case**, said that the Constitution could not be amended by Parliament if the changes affect basic issues such as fundamental rights. The **Kesavanada Bharati vs The State of Kerala Case** also was a matter of controversy. After the retirement of **Justice S.M Sikri**, Indira Gandhi indirectly appointed **A.N. Ray** as the Chief Justice of India by cornering three senior Judges. Soon after all the senior Judges resigned as a sign of protest against Indira Gandhi. Indira succeeded in turning the judiciary and also her rubber stamp. Justice **A.N. Ray** gave the judgement on the **Nationalisation of Banks, Privy Purse,** and many more in favour of the government of India. Conditions were getting worse day by day and effective protests were carried out by opposition parties during this period. The main epicentres were Bihar and Gujarat. In Gujarat, the students started protesting against the rising prices of food commodities in their mess bill. Due to this, early elections took place in Gujarat in 1975 and Congress was defeated. There was an intense protest in Bihar by the students and the entry of **Jayprakash Narayan** and the slogan **"Sampoorna Kranti"**, gave a massive boost to this protest and the protest spread nationwide. This protest was such a massive one that it deeply impact the common people and even the railways completely stop operations for more than a week! Nationwide agitations, rallies, bandhs, gheraos, strikes, etc. took place and even parliament rallies took place and a mass agitation was seen.

1975 was a turning point in Indian Politics. At this point, there was a complete paperwork process across the country. There was nothing like digitalization in the country and everything was as slow as a snail if we talk about government offices, for once, even a snail wonders whether anyone walks slower than me. In India, the ballot system was used till 2001 and after that **Electronic Voting machines** completely replaced the ballot system. In the ballot system of voting, it was easy to manipulate the votes, and malpractices were carried out. The same thing was carried out in the 1971 General Elections. According to the **Election Commission of India's Repor**t on the **Fifth General Elections** in India 1971-72, on March 20, 1971, Blitz tabloid published from Bombay (now Mumbai) claimed that ballot papers could have been chemically treated to alter electoral results and also described the modus operandi. a certain percentage of ballot papers in 200 to 250 of the 518 parliamentary constituencies that went to the polls were chemically treated and stamped with invisible ink, which became visible on the **'Calf and Cow'** symbol of Indira Gandhi's **Indian National Congress (R)** after 72 hours and the actual stamp put in by voters disappeared. There were also charges of a Russian connection. It was also claimed that the chemically treated ballot papers were printed in and imported from the Soviet Union. Allahabad High Court on 12 June 1975 gave a judgment that the 1971 General Elections were subjected to electoral malpractice and **Justice Jaganmohan Lal Sinha** declared Indira Gandhi's candidature invalid. Now she was dismissed as an MP and could not remain as a country's Prime Minister for more than 6 months! Supreme Court passed a partial stay on the orders of the High Court, which means she can remain as MP but won't be allowed to participate in parliament proceedings. Nationwide protest again started in the country and this time, complete opposition was on one stage demanding the resignation of Madam Prime Minister as the orders were all "**illegal orders of illegal Prime Minister**" and this time, the fire was very enormous and even more detrimental than the previous ones but Madam denied to resign.

❦❦❦

FOUR

THE DARK ERA OF INDIAN DEMOCRACY

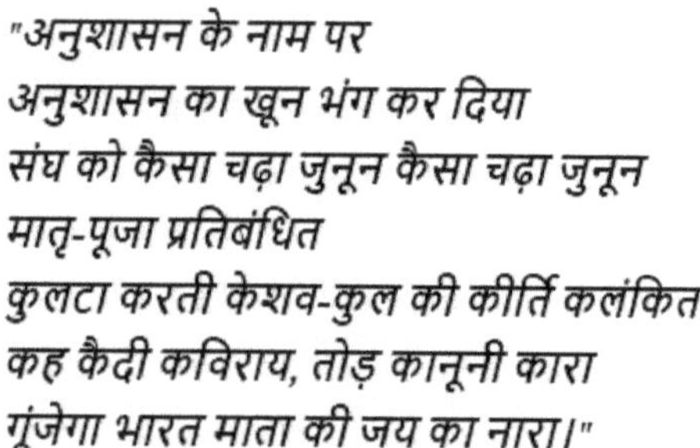

After resolving a procedural matter, President **Fakhruddin Ali Ahmed** declared a state of **internal emergency** upon the prime minister's advice on **25 June 1975**, just a few minutes before the clock struck midnight.

> *"भाइयों और बहनों, राष्ट्रपति जी ने आपातकाल की घोषणा की है। इससे आतंकित होने का कोई कारण नहीं है"*

and finally, an Emergency was imposed as per **Article 352 of the Constitution Of India**. After midnight, the electricity to all the central newspaper offices was disconnected. In the early morning, many leaders and workers of the opposition parties were arrested. The Cabinet was informed about it at a special meeting at 6 a.m. on 26 June, after all this had taken place. A nationwide arrest warrant was issued against all senior leaders of the country under such IPC sections, which were used for street gangsters. Even **Article 21** of the Constitution Of India suspended which gives the right to life in India. First, **Jayprakash Narayan** was arrested by Delhi Police while resting at **Gandhi Peace Foundation, Delhi** that night. **Atal Bihari Vajpayee, Lal Krishna Advani, Arun Jaitley, Vijayaraje Scindia, Raj Narain, Morarji Desai, Charan Singh**, and other protest leaders were immediately arrested. Organisations like the **Rashtriya Swayamsevak Sangh (RSS), Jamaat-e-Islami**, and some political parties were banned. Congress leaders who dissented against the Emergency declaration and amendment to the constitution, such as **Mohan Dharia** and **Chandra Shekhar**, resigned from their government and party positions and were after that arrested and placed under detention. Members of regional opposition parties such as DMK also found themselves arrested. Ultimately, now no one can become a hurdle in Indira's political race. Now she can remain in power until she wants to be. Even the ministry of **I.K. Gujral** (Information and Broadcasting Minister, 1975) was changed when he was asked to report to Sanjay Gandhi about the broadcasting details on **Doordarshan Television** and he refused to do so. To create a positive impact on the public, she announced a **'20-point' economic programme** to increase agricultural and industrial production, improve public services and fight poverty and illiteracy. **Sanjay Gandhi** declared his five-point programme was promoting literacy, family planning, tree planting, eradicating casteism, and dowry abolition. Later during the Emergency, the two projects merged into a **twenty-five-point programme**. Indira Gandhi was a prime minister only by law but not in reality, decision-making authority was Sanjay Gandhi. And here starts the rise of Sanjay Gandhi. Elections of all the state governments and even the General Elections were to be held in 1976.

Meanwhile, the 42nd Amendment was bought by Indira Gandhi during the Emergency. This amendment endeavoured to reduce the powers of the Supreme Court and High Court, alter the Preamble and some of the claws of the Indian Constitution and also the fundamental duties of Indian citizens towards the nation. On 31 July 1980, in its judgement on **Minerva Mills v. Union of India,** the Supreme Court declared two provisions of the 42nd Amendment as unconstitutional which prevent any constitutional amendment from being "called in question in any Court on any ground" and accord precedence to the Directive Principles of State Policy over the Fundamental Rights of individuals respectively. The Emergency era had been widely unpopular, and the 42nd Amendment was the most controversial issue. The clampdown on civil liberties and widespread abuse of human rights by police angered the public. In a speech in the Lok Sabha on 27 October 1976, Gandhi claimed that the amendment "is responsive to the aspirations of the people, and reflects the realities of the present time and the future". The 42nd Amendment changed the description of India from a **"sovereign democratic republic"** to a **"sovereign, socialist secular democratic republic",** and also changed the words "unity of the nation" to "unity and integrity of the nation". This is a knowing blunder and a genuine attempt to kill the constitution. Indira Gandhi promised to improve the standard of living of the people of India. She tried to do so by making the commodities cheaper but due to international sanctions, this was not a long-term benefit. This was only possible before the emergency because of the RBI 6% ceiling on annual money supply growth months and natural situations like record monsoons, which led to the record harvest of grains, reduced commodity demands and low worker wages and bonuses. Between 1 April and 6 October 1976, the wholesale price index rose by 10%, in which the price of rice rose by 8.3%, groundnut oil rose by 48%, and the prices of industrial raw materials as a group grew by 29.3%. Tax policy was amended and different slabs were created according to the same and it exempted the payers earning INR 6000-8000. Payers with an income of INR 8000-16000 were taxed INR 250 (approx.). Wealth taxes were reduced to 2.5% and 66% tax on the payers earning INR 1,00,000. This resulted in a decrease in the yearly revenue of the Indian Government and therefore expenditure on basics like social, education and health were reduced.

Apart from this, forced sterilisation was initiated by Sanjay Gandhi, due to which he was highly criticised. This can be called a disputed matter. Some intellectuals believe this is a blunder while some believe this is a step towards population control due to high pressure from **United Nations**, the **United States and World Bank**. Some intellectuals slam the officials for implementing this wrong, while some slam Sanjay Gandhi for the same. In 1976–1977, the program led to **8.3 million sterilizations**, most of them forced, up from 2.7 million the previous year. The bad publicity led many 1977 governments to stress that family planning is entirely voluntary. Several Demolitions took place in Delhi under the city's urban renewal programme and beautification. In total, 7,00,000 people in Delhi were displaced due to the demolitions in Delhi. Not only in Delhi but these activities were also carried out in other states such as Maharashtra, Bihar, Haryana and many others. Even Kishore Da was banned in the country during the Emergency period. Kishore Da was asked to sing a song for the Congress campaign and refused to do so, so an unofficial ban was put on Kishore Da's songs from All India Radio and Doordarshan until the end of the Emergency. Destruction of the slum and low-income housing in the Turkmen

Gate and Jama Masjid area of Old Delhi was also criticized. Not only in Delhi but these types of destructions were also carried out in other states of Delhi such as **Madhya Pradesh, Maharashtra, Bihar and Haryana**.

During the Emergency, several resistance movements like "Democracy Bachao Andolan", organisations like RSS and political parties like **CPI(M)** protested against this political disaster. Democracy Bachao Morcha was a movement carried out under **Shiromani Akali Dal**. They also stated that The question before us is not whether Indira Gandhi should continue to be prime minister or not. The point is whether democracy in this country is to survive or not. Complete RSS was banned during the emergency and the police detained several Swayamsevaks. **Nanaji Deshmukh, Madanlal Khurana, Narendra Modi, Atal Bihari Vajpayee, Lal Krishna Advani, Arun Jaitely, Subramanyam Swamy,** etc. were arrested. Some of them like Narendra Modi and Subramanyam Swamy managed to escape from jail and Atalji also got relief due to his health issues. The RSS 'Document of Surrender, was also confirmed by Subramanian Swamy in his article: "...I must add that not all in the RSS were in a surrender mode...But a tearful Muley told me in early November 1976 that I had better escape abroad again since the RSS had finalized the Document of Surrender to be signed at end of January 1977, and that on Mr Vajpayee's insistence, I would be sacrificed to appease an irate Indira and a fulminating Sanjay....". Even CPI(M) leaders like **Sitaram Yechury** and **Pinaryi Vijayan** were detained.

So finally on 21 March 1977, the Emergency was withdrawn from the country and thus a so-called **"democracy"** was back in India. Indira Gandhi resigned and called fresh General Elections in India in 1977. Some of her supporters say that Indira realised her mistake but some say that Indira's motive behind the emergency was fulfilled. Even after her resignation as Prime Minister, many of the opposition leaders were still in the prison. People lost their faith in Indira Gandhi and this election was a test for Indira Gandhi for her decision. In this election, **Janata Party** won 298 seats and Congress only 154. Congress Party failed to win even a single seat from Uttar Pradesh and Bihar even Indira Gandhi lost Rae Bareli's seat. And thus, **Morarji Desai** became the first non-congress Prime Minister Of India. Finally, Morarji's dream of becoming the Prime Minister since 1964, was completed in 1977.

See, all have different opinions about the same. Many books have been penned by several dignitaries, foreign journalists and some of the best intellectuals in India. Some favoured this situation and some severely opposed it. The public already answered and cast their opinion in the 1977 General Elections. Mostly all political ideologies consider this a wrong decision and it was. The **forced sterilisation** process carried out by Sanjay Gandhi was wrong. There was a need to control the growing population of India but the process of implementation was completely wrong. Talking about the positive vibes during the emergency, the initial reaction towards the Emergency by the middle-class and lower-class people was positive. There was calm and tranquillity as the students returned to classrooms, and the demonstrations ended. The **Index of Industrial Production (IIP)** grew 6.1 per cent in 1975 and 10.4 per cent in 1976 over their previous year's levels, with basic metals, mining and quarrying, and electricity seeing the most growth over the two years. Exports rose from a value of Rs. 3,328.8 crores in 1974 to Rs. 4,042.8 crores in 1975 and Rs. 5,143.4 crores in 1976. Imports, on the other hand, stabilised and then even decreased. From 53 per cent in 1974, import growth slowed to 16.5 per cent in 1975 and 3.6 per cent in 1976. As far as labour unrest is concerned, the number of workdays lost to strikes fell precipitously, from 40.3 million workdays lost in 1974 to 21.9 million workdays in 1975 and just 12.8 million in 1976. Overall, the number of riots fell drastically in those two years, only to rise again in 1977. Looking at the government's expenditure during that time, the budget deficit widened during the Emergency. Gross fixed capital formation grew at 9.7 per cent and 12.6 per cent in 1975 and 1976, respectively, following years of poor growth.

ppp

FIVE

JANATA SARKAR – SHRI. MORARJI DESAI (1977-1979)

सिंहासन खाली करो "जनता" आ रही है

- श्री जयप्रकाश नारायण

As soon as the Janata Party won the elections, disputes started rising about the Prime Ministerial candidate. **Acharya Kriplani** and **Jayprakash Narayan** have to decide on the successor of Indira Gandhi out of three names- 1) **Morarji Desai**, 2) **Jagjivan Ram** and 3) **Chaudhary Charan Singh**. Jagjivan Ram was the one who introduced the Emergency in parliament and the case of Charan Singh, he was not even supported by his party members. Finally, Morarji Desai became the Prime Minister Of India after a struggle of 13 years. He assumed office on 24 March 1977 after the end of a **19-month emergency.** He previously served as the Chief Minister of the State Of Bombay. Also, He served in the Ministry of Home Affairs, finance and as Deputy Prime Minister Of India. He is the **oldest personto hold the office of prime minister, at 81**, in the history of Indian politics. Charan Singh and Jagjivan Ram had to satisfy with Home Ministry and Defence Ministry respectively and **Raj Narain** got Health Ministry. As soon as the Janata Government came to power, they started gathering the loss that occurred in the emergency period. To do so, an inquiry was appointed in 1977 by the Government of India under the leadership of **Justice Jayantilal Chotalal Shah**. First, several complaints were filed and later classified under different groups and on 29 September 1977, the commission started investigating. This commission was pressurized to do their work quickly and within the given deadline but not like other commissions that extend their deadlines. According to the reports, this commission was published in 3 volumes comprising a total of 525 pages describing the complete flashes of emergencies containing atrocities, torture, family planning, police firing, etc. This investigation also found that all the IAS officers across the country were practising forging records, fabrication of grounds of detention, ante-dating detention orders, and the callous disregard of the rights of detainees as regards revocation, parole, etc.

Desai tried to restore normal relations with China and Pakistan. He also refused to sign the non-nuclear proliferation policy despite continuous threats given by the US Congress about stopping the use of uranium for power plants. Janata Party was an amalgam of all the political parties who opposed during the emergencies. The only motto was to defeat Indira at any cost. Lots of different ideologies got together which led to clashes and thus the downfall of the Janata Government started. Some corruption allegations were put against **Kanti Desai** (Morarji's son), Charan Singh lifted the matter and was asked to set up an investigation for this case and clashes started increasing between both. Charan Singh wanted to set up fast track court for fast and speedy decisions for all the cases against Indira Gandhi and Morarji denied to do so. Gradually, Charan Singh started making statements against his party that too publically. Thus Morarji asked Raj Narain and Charan Singh for their resignation, and both resigned from their respective posts. After the resignation of these leaders, this coalition government started weakening. And thus, Indira Gandhi and Sanjay Gandhi got a chance to topple the governments. It is said that many secret meetings were held between Raj Narain and Sanjay Gandhi during this time and a big conspiracy started to take shape. Days after, Morarji Desai invited Charan Singh and asked him to join the cabinet. Charan Singh was sworn in as Deputy Prime Minister of India. Indira Gandhi won the by-elections from Chikmagalur Constituency in Karnataka but the government strongly started taking action and making false allegations against Indira Gandhi in the parliament as if their only motto is to boycott Indira Gandhi as more as possible e.g. " Four Hens and Two Eggs" Allegation. I would only say, "जनता समझदार है भाई". Janata Party Government started restoring all the amendments which were done in Emergency time. Now the real countdown started beginning. No Confidence Motion started against the Janata Government in 1979. Soon, all supporters of Raj Narain and Charan Singh started giving resignations and gradually ministers also started giving resignations. Lastly, Morarji Desai also resigned from his position and Janata Party ended........

▷▷▷

"Forgotten Prime Minister"- Shri. Chaudhary Charan Singh

""The true India resides in its villages."

Finally, an attempt to topple the Janata Government got successful and now both the congress came together to support Charan Singh in 1979 but the truce did not last long, and a mutiny reduced the government to a minority. Indira Gandhi took back the support from the government and Charan Singh resigned just **23 days** after he took the office. Though he continued being a caretaker Prime Minister Of India for the next 179 days.

SIX

SWEEPING THE POLLS- INDIRA GANDHI TERM 3 (1981-1984*)

The Janata Party, an amalgam of socialists and nationalists, split in 1979 when several coalition members including the **Bharatiya Lok Dal** and several members of the **Socialist Party** withdrew support for the government. Subsequently, Desai lost a vote of confidence in parliament and resigned. Charan Singh, who had retained some partners of the Janata alliance, was sworn in as Prime Minister in June 1979. the INC promised to support Singh in parliament but later backed out just two days before the Govt was scheduled to prove its majority on the floor of Lok Sabha. Charan Singh, forced to resign, called for elections in January 1980 and is the only Prime Minister of India never to have obtained the confidence of Parliament. In the run-up to the general elections, Indira Gandhi's leadership faced a formidable political challenge from a galaxy of regional satraps and prominent leaders of the Janata party like **Satyendra Narayan Sinha and Karpuri Thakur** in Bihar, **Ramakrishna Hegde** in Karnataka, **Sharad Pawar** in Maharashtra, Devi Lal in Haryana & **Biju Patnaik** in Orissa. Janata Party contested the election with **Jagjivan Ram** as its Prime Ministerial candidate. However, the internal feud between Janata Party leaders and the political instability in the country worked in favour of Indira Gandhi's Congress (I), which reminded voters of the strong government of Indira Gandhi during campaigning. In the ensuing elections, the INC won 353 seats and the Janata Party just 31 seats, with Charan Singh's **Janata Party (Secular)** taking 41. The Janata Party alliance continued to split over the subsequent year.

Indira swept the 1980 General Elections and swore in again as the Prime Minister Of India. Indira faced many challenges this year. Though she won the 1980 General Elections with a hefty margin of votes, she lost her son, Sanjay **Gandhi**. On 23 June 1980, Sanjay Gandhi died in a plane crash near Safdarjung Airport. Sanjay Gandhi was one of the prominent faces of Indian Politics and his demise led to the entry of a new face in Indian Politics, i.e. **Rajiv Gandhi**.

In India, till the 1970s there was a dominance of Ambassador and Padmini Cars and there was not a single car that a middle-class family could afford. In 1981, Indira Gandhi established Maruti Udyog Limited (formerly Maruti Motors Limited which was nationalised in 1981 as a tribute to Sanjay Gandhi) to manufacture Make-In-India cars which would be affordable to all categories. So joint venture bids from automobile companies around the world were invited from which Suzuki of Japan was selected as the partner. The company launched its first Indian-manufactured car in 1983 and the first car was handed over to **Harpal Singh**. Today also he is using this car and has maintained it very well. There was a massive demand for Maruti Cars back in 1984 and today also, this company holds more than 42% of the automobile market share as of 2022.

The context for domestic policy during this stage was the dominance of the Congress Party and an increasingly authoritarian style of government by Indira Gandhi. The most critical foreign policy context was one or two changes in the Cold War. The USA was providing Pakistan with military and moral weapons and making India's arch-enemy one of its main allies (against the Soviet Union). At the same time, an ideological and power political rift opened up between Beijing and Moscow. This subsequently led to a rapprochement between the **People's Republic of China** and the **USA.** In this phase, there was the first turnaround in Indian foreign policy, which can be traced back to both personal and structural origins. Indira Gandhi leaned more obviously than the previous leadership towards the Soviet Union as a critical international partner (and distanced herself even further from the USA). She represented more clearly than the previous leadership a policy of regional domination, which had as its objective the hegemony of India in South Asia (cf. Rothermund 2003).

The relationship between India and the Soviet Union deepened during Indira Gandhi's rule. The support of the Soviets with arms supplies, and the use of the veto at the United Nations, helped India win and consolidate its victory over Pakistan in the **1971 Bangladesh liberation war**. Subsequently, the Soviet Union became the leading arms supplier during the rule of Indira Gandhi. Indira Gandhi was a staunch supporter of Palestinians in the Arab–Israeli conflict and was critical of the Middle East diplomacy sponsored by the United States. India under Indira Gandhi viewed Israel as a religious state, analogous to her adversary, Pakistan. Indian diplomats also hoped to win Arab support in countering Pakistan in Kashmir. India's pro-Arab policy had mixed success. During the Indo-Pakistani War of 1971, while the progressive Arab regimes in Egypt, Syria, and Algeria chose to remain neutral, the conservative pro-American Arab Monarchies in Jordan, Saudi Arabia, Kuwait, and the United Arab Emirates openly supported Pakistan.

"Operation Blue Star"

Indira strengthened the International stand of India as well as the economic conditions of India. Everything was all fine till 1984 but Indira Gandhi faced her own mistake committed in 1977- Yes! I am signalling towards **"Operation Blue Star"**. The story starts in 1977 when Indira Gandhi lost the General Assembly and State Assembly Elections. Congress Party lifted **Damdami Taksal** against the **Shiromani Akali Dal** in Punjab and appointed **Jarnail Singh Bhindranwale** on the suggestions of Sanjay Gandhi and **Gyani Zail Singh**. Clashes took place between two Sikh communities- **Nirankari Sikh** and **Amritdhari Sik**h in which 13 Amritdhari Sikhs lost their lives and legal cases were filed in this matter. In 1980, **Baba Gurbachan Singh**, leader of Nirankari Sikh was shot dead by **Ranjit Singh** after a few days of Baisakhi. In the 1980 General Elections, Bhindranwale openly came into public and campaigned for Indira Gandhi. In this period, Congress won both the State as well as Central Elections. Gyani Zail Singh was promoted to the Ministry Of Home Affairs in Indira Gandhi's Government and with the same, **Darbara Singh** was promoted to Chief Minister Of Punjab. Meanwhile. **Lala Jagat Narain**, founder of **Punjab Kesari** used to target the state government and various activities of Bhindranwale and publish such staunch articles due to which, many devout Sikhs were angry with him. On 9 September 1981, Lala Jagat Narain was shot dead and on 15 September, Bhindranwale was arrested from Amritsar. But he was finely released saying that **"there is no evidence against Bhindranwale"** which was declared by the then Home Minister Shri Gyani Zail Singh, that too in the parliament! Several allegations were made against the Congress Party by the opposition that the Congress Party is indirectly supporting Bhindranwale and due to which he is freely roaming in the country with his Sikh bodyguards! Meanwhile, he openly started praising Indira Gandhi and his government for all the past instances that occurred with him! And thus, the demand for Khalistan took momentum and Bhindranwale declared a massive protest in Delhi. India hosted **ASIAD Games** during this duration of time due to which, security was tightened in Delhi and borders were completely sealed for security purposes. Strict checking was conducted on every vehicle passing by. Even MLAs, MPs, Air Chief Marshals, BSF Officers, and Police vehicles were also strictly checked. During this period, nearly 1500 people were arrested and Bhindranwale took the opportunity and started spreading hatred amongst the people. Terrorism, Murders, and illegal activities were encouraged in Punjab and Bhindranwale's terror spread all over Punjab. Chief Minister Darbara Singh begged him for the body of DIG **Avtar Singh Atwal** who was shot dead by a gunman outside **Darbar Sahib**. Thus you can imagine the situation. Darbara Singh suggested Indira Gandhi take military actions in Punjab, but Gyani Zail Singh denied it. Terrorism increased in Punjab and the situation became more worst here. The situation stood up like Gyani Zail Singh vs Darbara Singh rather than controlling the situation, it was becoming worst day by day. Indira Gandhi tried to make a way out of it by promoting Gyani Zail Singh as the President of India, but the situation didn't control. Several Hindu Genocide started in Punjab. Lastly, Indira Gandhi dismissed Darbara Singh's Government and imposed presidential rule. Hindu Genocide continued in Punjab despite of President's Rule in the state! On 15 December 1983, Bhindranwale captured the **"Akaal Takht"** which has significant importance in the Sikh religion as well as politics. Bhindranwale challenged Indira Gandhi saying that-

""We are like a matchstick, it is made of wood and it is cold, but if you light it, flames will come out"*"*

Several talks took place between the government and Bhindranwale but all failed. Hindu Genocide continued and this impacted also other states where Sikhs were killed and Gurudwaras were demolished, Many reports came to the government regarding mass killings of Hindus which were publically declared. Now finally, Indira has to take the decisions as early as possible. Finally, On 1 June 1984, Punjab was officially handed over to the army and the very next day, Indira Gandhi appealed for the last time through Doordarshan and nothing was impacted through her appeal as if the appeal was made only for the sake of formality. All the telephone lines were cut down in Punjab, Borders were sealed, and Journalists and reporters were removed from Amritsar. Bhindranwale firmly said that he would fight till the last and Operation Blue Star started. Under the leadership of **Lt. Gen Kuldip Singh Brar**, On 3rd June 1984, Army surrounded the Golden Temple Complex and just before the commencement of the Operation, Lt. Gen. Kuldip Singh Brar said that-

> *"The action is not against the Sikhs or the Sikh religion; it is against terrorism. If anyone amongst them has strong religious sentiments or other reservations and does not wish to take part in the operation, he can opt-out, and it will not be held against him."*

On 4 and 5 June, messages asking pilgrims to leave the temple were played over loudspeakers. However, in 2017 the Amritsar District and Sessions Judge **Gurbir Singh** gave a ruling which stated that there was no evidence that the Indian army provided warnings for pilgrims to leave the temple complex before commencing their assault. The army began bombarding the historic **Ramgarhia Bunga**, the water tank, and other fortified positions with Ordnance **QF 25-pounder artillery**. After destroying the outer defences laid by **Shabeg Singh**, the army moved tanks and APCs onto the road separating the Guru Nanak Niwas building. The army helicopters spotted the massive movements, and General K. Sunderji sent tanks and APCs to meet them. The artillery and small arms firing stopped for a while and **Gurcharan Singh Tohra**, former head of **Shiromani Gurudwara Prabhandak Committee**, was sent to negotiate with Bhindranwale for his surrender. He was, however, unsuccessful and the firing resumed. As of 5 June, pilgrims who had reached the temple on 3 June were still present hiding in rooms. In one room 40-50, persons were huddled together including a six-month-old child during the army's assault. A female survivor of the assault stated that the army asked people to leave their hiding spots and guaranteed safe passage and water; she recalled seeing the dead bodies of pilgrims who answered the announcements lying in the Parikrama the next morning. Massive destructions took place and even the Akaal Takht got damaged. Many casualties took place but finally on 7 June 1984 Bhindranwale's dead body was discovered and officially, the operation ended on 10 June 1984. An attempt was made to kill Gyani Zail Singh on the temple's premises when he visited Golden Temple failed; unfortunately, one of his bodyguards was injured.

According to Lt. Gen. Kuldip Singh Brar, around **83** soldiers lost their lives, **248** were injured, and **492** terrorists of Bhindranwale were dead. Many harmful weapons were seized from the complex, This Operation Blue Star succeeded but the situation in Punjab didn't control and even became worse. It is said that-

यदि बीज बोया जाए, पानी दिया जाए, खाद दी जाए तो वृक्ष अवश्य ही बढ़ता है और यदि वृक्ष काट भी दिया जाए फिर भी उसकी जड़े बनी रहती है

This incident could have been prevented if the government had taken the right steps at the right time. The chapter started for political gains for Congress in Punjab and later resulted in massive destruction. Though, political games were played despite this situation. Even the President Of India, the supreme head of the army was unaware of all the incidents. This incident shocked India deeply and by this, the countdown of Indira Gandhi was started. Gandhi's intellectuals suggested that she should remove all the Sikh bodyguards from her convoy but she denied doing so and she was correct in her opinion.

At about 9:20 a.m. Indian Standard Time, on 31 October 1984, Gandhi was on her way to be interviewed by British actor Peter Ustinov, who was filming a documentary for Irish television. She was accompanied by Constable Narayan Singh, personal security officer Rameshwar Dayal and Gandhi's secretary, R. K. Dhawan. She was walking through the garden of the Prime Minister's Residence at No. 1 Safdarjung Road in New Delhi towards the neighbouring 1 Akbar Road office.

Gandhi passed a wicket gate guarded by **Satwant Singh** and **Beant Singh**, and the two men opened fire. Beant Singh fired three rounds into her abdomen from his .38 (9.7 mm) revolver then Satwant fired 30 rounds from his Sterling sub-machine gun after she had fallen to the ground. Both men then threw down their weapons and Beant said,

"I have done what I had to do. You do what you want to do."

In the next six minutes, Border Police officers Tarsem Singh Jamwal and Ram Saran captured and killed Beant, while Satwant was arrested by Gandhi's other bodyguards and an accomplice trying to escape; he was seriously wounded. Satwant Singh was hanged in 1989 with their accomplice Kehar Singh.

Indira Gandhi was then admitted to the **All India Institute Of Medical Sciences, New Delhi**. She was declared dead at 2:20 p.m.

The postmortem examination was conducted by a team of doctors headed by Tirath Das Dogra, who stated that 30 bullets had struck Gandhi from a Sterling sub-machine gun and a revolver. The assailants had fired 33 bullets at her, of which 30 had hit; 23 had passed through her body, while 7 remained inside. Dogra extracted bullets to establish the identity of the weapons and to correlate each weapon with the bullets recovered by ballistic examination. The bullets were matched to the weapons at CFSL Delhi. The Indian government ordered a national mourning from November 1 to November 12 with flags half-masted and cancelled entertainment and cultural events and offices closed for several days. Pakistan declared three days of mourning and Bulgaria declared a day of national mourning. Gandhi's body was taken in a gun carriage through Delhi roads on the morning of 1 November to Teen Murti Bhavan, where her father stayed and where she lay in state. She was cremated with full state honours on 3 November near Raj Ghat in an area named **Shakti Sthal.**

Shakti Sthal

मैं आज यहाँ हू कल शायद यहाँ ना रहु. मेरा लम्बा जीवन रहा है और मुझे इस बात का गर्व है की मैंने अपना पूरा जीवन अपने लोगो की सेवा में बिताया है. मैं अपनी आखरी सांस तक ऐसा करती रहूंगी और जब मैं मरूंगी तो मेरा खून का एक एक कतरा भारत को मजबूत करने में लगेगा

Enter Caption

ᐅᐅᐅ

SEVEN

YOUNG MAN- SHRI. RAJIV GANDHI (1984-1989)

"Better a brain drain than a brain in the drain."

It was previously cleared that the only successor of Indira Gandhi stands his elder son Rajiv Gandhi and all the party members of congress agreed to the same. But, seeing the current situation in India at that time, Sonia Gandhi begged and urged Rajiv Gandhi not to succeed her mother. But Rajiv Gandhi denied and assumed office and succeeded Indira Gandhi on the day of her assassination on 31 October 1984. At 40, he became the youngest Prime Minister Of India. The same day, Delhi went on fire. Several Sikhs were openly killed. Cases of these instances went on increasing. The government deployed the **Central Reserve Police Force (CRPF)** in the city, but things worsened. The government was engaged in covering all the incidents. The army was also deployed on the ground but was ordered not to fire. Things became so worse that the dead bodies of Sikhs were coming in the train and were pulled out from the trolley. This went on for 3 days. Thousands of Sikhs were killed and this turned out to be a massacre. It was like the government was just watching this drama as if this was revenge for the assassination of Indira Gandhi. Suddenly after 3 days, this was finished! Isn't it sound like a pre-planned event? As per the reports, about 3,000 Sikhs in Delhi were killed in violence soon after the assassination of Indira Gandhi.

Anti-Sikh Riots, 1984Samvel Ghulyan, CC BY-SA 4.0 <https://creativecommons.org/licenses/by-sa/4.0>, via Wikimedia Commons

Soon after 1 month, India underwent its next General Elections though the vote in Assam and Punjab was delayed until 1985 due to ongoing fighting. The elections were a landslide victory for the Indian National Congress of Rajiv Gandhi which won 404. The **Telugu Desam Party** of **N. T. Rama Rao**, a regional political party from the state of Andhra Pradesh, was the second largest party, winning 30 seats, thus achieving the distinction of becoming the first regional party to become a national opposition party. Voting was held immediately after the assassination of Indira Gandhi and the 1984 anti-Sikh riots in November and most of India supported Congress. The 1984 elections were the last in which a single party won a majority of seats until 2014, and the only time to date in which a party won more than 400 seats.

Rajiv Gandhi assumed office for the second time and **"With great power comes great responsibility"**. Already during his previous tenure, Anti Sikh Riots took place in India and now many more are waiting ahead. Rajiv Gandhi excluded **Pranab Mukherjee** and **Ghani Khan Choudhary** from his cabinet. He use to frequently reshuffle the cabinet and fire the ministers who do not use to work to the mark. Rajiv Gandhi was a young leader, he tried to shift India towards the 21st Century by introducing new technologies to the country like computers, Mobile Phones and much more. People appreciated his ideas and his working method but the opposition used to slam for the same. During his tenure, **Anti Defamation Rule** was passed in the parliament. A funny as well as the interesting incident of Indian Politics I want to share, which lead to this law. In 1967, Haryana went to its State General Elections in which, Congress Party won 48 seats and proved their majority. **Gaya Lal**, one of the winners from **Hassanpur Constituency** Of **Haryana State**. He fought as an independent candidate for this seat and won by a majority, joined the Indian National Congress, and thereafter he changed parties thrice in a fortnight, first by politically defecting from the Indian National Congress to the United Front, then counter defecting back to INC, and then counter-counter-defected within nine hours to United Front again. When Gaya Lal quit the United Front and join the INC, then INC leader Rao Birendra Singh who had engineered Gaya Lal's defection to INC, brought Gaya Lal to a press conference at Chandigarh and declared "Gaya Ram was now Aya Ram". and the phrase became popular as-

"Aaya Ram Gaya Ram"

According to this law, an elected Member of Parliament or legislative assembly could not join an opposition party until the next election. Many such defections occurred during the 1980s as elected leaders of the Congress party joined opposition parties.

A very popular incident took place during that time, which took immense momentum-the **"Shah Bano Case" (Mohommed Ahmed Khan VS Begum Shah Bano)**. Shah Bano was married to **Mohd. Ahmed Khan** in 1932. They have sons and 2 daughters. Shah Bano's husband had asked her to move to a separate residence in 1975. After 3 years, when Shah Bano asked for her alimony, she was denied by Mohd. Ahmed Khan and gave her a divorce. **Shah Bano** went to court and filed a claim for maintenance for herself and her five children under Section 123 of the Code of Criminal Procedure, 1973. District Magistrate Court and High Court passed judgement in favour of Shah Bano and thus the case reached the Apex Court Of India. The 5-judge bench headed by **Y.V Chandrachud** passed the judgement in favour of Shah Bano and said that Shah Bano is entitled to alimony of Rs 500 per month by her husband. And from here, the Apex Court suggested the current government for Uniform Civil Code across the country. **All India Muslim Personal Law Board** opposed the judgement passed by the Apex Court and protests started in the country. Rajiv Gandhi tried to convince the community regarding the judgement of the Supreme Court but he failed to do so. Lastly, in 1986, The Government passed **"The Muslim Women Protection Of Rights and Divorce Act 1986"** according to which, Muslim women can get mahr and alimony only for 3 months. And thus all the rights of Muslim women were finished. This bill faced many protests in the parliament but was passed due to the complete majority in both houses. Former Law Minister of India, **Ram Jethmalani**, called the Act **"retrogressive obscurantism for short-term minority populism"**.

Rajiv Gandhi's government also focused on the economic policies of India and as a young mind and a man of new-era thinking, he tried to liberalise the Indian Economy. The government intended to establish large-scale industry, increase foreign investments in the country, and increase employment he also did so by providing incentives to the corporates but rural and tribal people protested because they saw them as **"pro-rich"** and **"pro-city"** reforms. Even the opposition opposed the same. Rajiv Gandhi was a man of modern thinking. He increased government support for science, technology and associated industries, and reduced import quotas, taxes and tariffs on technology-based industries, especially computers, airlines, defence and telecommunications. He introduced **National Policy on Education** to modernise and expand high-quality and higher education institutions in India. He also put forth the concept of the Navoday Vidhyalaya System in India, which aims to impart free education to the rural areas of India from grades 6 to 12. He introduced reduced the Licence Raj after 1990, allowing businesses and individuals to purchase capital, consumer goods and import without bureaucratic restrictions.

On 30 April 1986, About 200 Sikh militants entered the Golden Temple and occupied the place. Under the leadership of **DGP Of Punjab State Commander Julio Riberio**, **300 NSG** and **700 BSF** troops entered the premises of **Sri Harmandir Sahib**, which lasts 8 hours and finally captured all the militants. One person was killed and two were injured. The second part of this Operation began on 9 May 1988. The Operation was commanded by the DGP of the Punjab Police **Kanwar Pal Singh Gill**. The operation was successful. Around 200 militants surrendered and 41 were killed in this operation. During the news channel, the media was allowed to report the site. Kirtan was resumed at the Golden Temple on 23 May 1988 after a two-week break during this operation. **Operation Black Thunder** was far more successful with the blockade tactics paying dividends and has been credited with breaking the back of the Sikh separatist movement. Soon after this operation, the Indian Government banned the use of religious shrines for political and military purposes and increased penalties for the possession and use of illegal weapons, as part of its strategy to fight extremism in the Punjab region.

Gandhi employed former Rockwell International executive Sam Pitroda as his public information infrastructure and innovation adviser. During Gandhi's time in office, public sector telecom companies **MTNL and VSNL** were developed. According to Pitroda, Gandhi's ability to resist pressure from multinational companies to abandon his plan to spread telecommunication services has been an important factor in India's development. According to the news website Oneindia, "About 20 years ago telephones were considered to be a thing for the use of the rich, but credit goes to Rajiv Gandhi for taking them to the rural masses". Pitroda also said their plan to expand India's telephone network succeeded because of Gandhi's political support. According to Pitroda, by 2007 they were "adding six million phones every month". Gandhi's government also allowed the import of fully assembled motherboards, which led to the price of computers being reduced. According to some commentators, the seed for the information technology (IT) revolution was also planted during Rajiv Gandhi's time.

Gandhi's prime ministership marked an increase in the insurgency in northeast India. **Mizo National Front** demanded independence for Mizoram. In 1987, Gandhi addressed this problem; Mizoram and Arunachal Pradesh were given the status of states that were earlier union territories. Gandhi also ended the Assam Movement, which was launched by Assamese people to protest against the alleged illegal migration of Bangladeshi Muslims and immigration of other Bengalis to their state, which reduced the Assamese to a minority there. He signed the Assam Accord on 15 August 1985. According to the accord, foreigners who came to the state between 1951 and 1961 were given full citizenship but those who arrived there between 1961 and 1971 did not get the right to vote for the next ten years.

"Bofors"- This word played a very significant role in Indian Politics. A scam of Rs. **65 Crore** changed the upcoming political scenario of India. On 24 March 1986, a $285 million contract was signed between the **Government of India** and Swedish arms company Bofors for supplying Howitzer field guns. But the scam was the result of internal politics. The story starts when Rajiv Gandhi was sworn in as the Prime Minister Of India and **Vishwanath Pratap Singh** became the Finance Minister Of India. Being a Finance Minister, he did a good job of tracking tax evasion and raided a lot of businessmen for the same. But he was transferred to the Ministry Of Defence. Some believe that due to raids, many of the corporates were angry due to these activities and due to this, his ministry transferred. Some believed there was a need for a strict leader like V.P Singh in the defence sector and some believe that the ministry was transferred due to the rising stature of V.P Singh in the party. **Fairfax Investigation** was given the task to investigate the issue and all the internal talks of the ministry got leaked. Several allegations were made against V.P Singh saying that there is a conspiracy planned to degrade the image of the government. Singh clarified the differences in the cabinet in commissions taken by Indian agents in the **HDW submarine deal**. Rajiv Gandhi soon gave the orders to finalise the HDW submarine deal without prior discussions with his cabinet. V.P Singh got a telegram stating that there is some corruption in this deal. He ordered the investigation without the prior permission of V.P Singh. He was repeatedly alleged by his party and so he finally resign from the government on 12 April 1987. After 4 days, a message was broadcasted on Sweden Radio stations stating that Bofors has paid Indians and others to take home their biggest deal. Swedish radio alleged that 64 Crores were paid as a commission to Indian agents. When this deal was done, the ministry was under Rajiv Gandhi itself. Allegations didn't stop there, it went on surrounding Rajiv Gandhi. **Arun Nehru, V.C. Shukla,** and **Arif Mohammad Khan** were expelled from the party. V.P Singh resigned from the Rajyasabha and then was removed from the Congress Party. Arun Singh, MoS Defence also demanded the investigation but Rajiv Gandhi denied and so, Arun Singh also resigned from the Party. Rajiv Gandhi's Government got stuck in this quagmire. Day by day this case used to get a new twist, everyday new evidence, new names, entry of Swiss bank, the diary of Oderburg, involvement of s **Ottavio Quattrocchi,** etc.

Due to this scandal, Rajiv Gandhi Government was severely alleged from all sides, and also Congress Party lost the **1989 General Elections**. Though it remained the single largest party with 197 seats in the parliament.

On 29 July 1987, a treaty was signed between India and Sri Lanka in which Sri Lankan Government agreed to provide more rights and freedom to Tamil Hindus in the country and return, Tamil Hindus have to keep their weapon down. **Liberation Tigers Of Tamil Eelam (LTTE)** wanted to separate Tamil majority areas and want to establish a new country which was headed by **Velupillai Prabhakaran**. Prabhakaran just wanted independence from Sri Lanka and no treaty. The government of India tried to convince Prabhakaran but all talks failed. He just wanted an independent nation **"Eelam"**. Back in 1983, during Indira Gandhi, **Tamil Eelam Liberation Organization (TELO)** was trained and funded by the Government Of India to strengthen the Tamil groups in Sri Lanka. Now the question arises, why they were trained? After the Independence of Sri Lanka, Tamils were deprived of their fundamental rights and were marginalised and deprived. They were supremely dominated by Sinhalese people. Moreover, the Sri Lankan Government declared that Sinhala will be the only official language of Sri Lanka and even they declared Sri Lanka -the Buddhist Nation after the implementation of a new constitution in Sri Lanka. So due to these reasons, many rebellion groups started and the Indian Government was forced to help the Tamil groups of India in Sri Lanka. **Anti-Tamil Riots** started in Sri Lanka after LTTE came into action by attacking the army officials of Sri Lanka. Lakhs of Tamil started migrating towards India. Civil War started in India and **Operation Poomalai** was carried out. Operation Poomalai was the codename assigned to a mission undertaken by the Indian Air Force for airdropping supplies over the besieged town of **Jaffna** in Sri Lanka on 4 June 1987 to support the Tamil Tigers during the Sri Lankan Civil War. India sent the Peacekeeping force and as per the treaty, Tamil groups surrendered. Things became worse in the upcoming days. Due to many misconceptions, LTTE became against Indian Peace Keeping Forces and a war-like situation raised in Sri Lanka. Meanwhile, after the change of power in Sri Lanka, the Sri Lankan Government stood with LTTE and started supplying weapons to them to fight against Indian Peace Keeping Force. After the change of power in India, V.P Singh, the then Prime Minister ordered the withdrawal of the Indian Peace Keeping Force from Sri Lanka. A total of 1248 soldiers were martyred in this situation. **Indian Peace Keeping Force** succeeded in reducing the effect of LTTE in Sri Lanka and also succeeded to normalise the situation to a greater extent. During the 1991 General Elections, there was a threat amongst LTTE that if Rajiv Gandhi came to power, he will take military action against LTTE. So LTTE targeted Rajiv Gandhi. When Rajiv reached a campaign rally in Sriperumbudur, he left his car and began walking towards the dais where he was to deliver a speech. Along the way, he was garlanded by many well-wishers, Indian National Congress workers and schoolchildren. The assassin, **Kalaivani Rajaratnam** (popularly known by her assumed names Thenmozhi Rajaratnam and Dhanu), approached and greeted him. She then bent down to touch his feet and detonated an RDX explosive-laden belt tucked below her dress at exactly 10:10 PM. Gandhi, his assassin and 14 others were killed in the explosion that followed, along with 43 others who were grievously injured. The assassination was caught on film by a local photographer, **Haribabu**, whose camera and film were found intact at the site despite him also dying in the blast. Rajiv Gandhi was cremated at **Veer Bhumi Delhi**. By this India lost a visionary leader, a man of modern ideologies.

Veer Bhumi, DelhiMohitSingh at English Wikipedia, CC BY-SA 3.0 <https://creativecommons.org/licenses/by-sa/3.0>, via Wikimedia Commons

"I am young, and I too have a dream. I dream of an India - strong, independent, self-reliant and in the front rank of the nations of the world in the service of mankind."
- Rajiv Gandhi

ԵԵԵ

EIGHT

RAJA BAHADUR SHRI. VISHWANATH PRATAP SINGH (1989-1990)

"I would be a disaster as a prime minister."

Vishwanath Pratap Singh

After allegations against **Amitabh Bachchan** in Bofors Case, he resigned as a Member Of Parliament from Allahabad and the seat got vacated. **Vishwanath Pratap Singh** contested as an independent candidate from the Allahabad seat against **Sunil Shastri**, son of **Lal Bahadur Shastri** of Congress. The entire opposition supported V.P

Singh and he won this seat. V.P Singh united some of the parties like **Jan Morcha, Janata Party, Lok Dal and Congress (S)**, and established **Janata Dal** to bring together all the centrist parties opposed to the Rajiv Gandhi government which, Singh was elected the President of the Janata Dal. V.P Singh stressed Bofors Deal in all his election rallies and programmes and declared that if he came to power, he would solve this matter and investigate the issue. In the 1989 General Elections, Congress was reduced to only 195 seats and emerged as the single largest party in the house. V.P. Singh's coalition front won 143 seats. He got support from the **Bharatiya Janata Party** and the **Left Front** and thus the complete coalition with support got 248 votes in favour and V.P Singh was elected as the Prime Minister Of India. When V.P. Singh came to power, he passed this complete to CBI for investigation. In 1993, Switzerland Court investigated this matter and found that **Quattrocchi** was the owner of **AE services**. In 1999, CBI filed a chargesheet against **Quattrocchi, Win Chadha, Rajiv Gandhi**, the defence secretary **S. K. Bhatnagar** and several others. Rajiv Gandhi's trial was cancelled as he was no more and Win Chadha and S. K. Bhatnagar died and so the investigation was also terminated. A supplementary chargesheet was filed against Srichand Hinduja, Gopichand Hinduja and Prakash Hinduja. In 2005, Delhi High Court dismissed the case against Hinduja Brothers. In 2013, **Ottavio Quattrocchi** died and so the case was dismissed. In 2011, a petition was filed by CBI to completely close Bofors Case, which the court approved and thus the "Bofors Case" concluded- Amitabh Bachchan and Rajiv Gandhi were found innocent. But the question remained intact; who is the bribe taker of Bofors?

Within a very few days of becoming the Prime Minister Of India, India faced one of the biggest Hindu Genocide- **The 1990 Kashmiri Pandit Exodus**. It starts back in 1984 during the elections when **Ghulam Mohammad Shah** broke about 13 MLAs of the **National Conference** and 26 MLAs of the Congress party and formed his government. There was complete anger among the people of Kashmir and protests started. The first incident of Kashmiri Pandits attacks came in 1986 from Anantnag where several Hindus were killed and temples were destroyed. The situation became worse and finally 7 March 1986, President Rule came to Kashmir for the first time since Independence. In 1987, the National Conference united with Congress and came to the power. In Kashmir, youths were trained with arms and ammunition and were being instigated. Radicalism started increasing slowly in the valley. In 1988, bars, cinemas, beauty parlours, and libraries were targeted. The kidnapping of the then Home Minister **Mufti Mohammad Sayeed's** daughter **Rubaiya Sayeed** led to the release of 4 terrorists of **JKLF**. The separatists gave the slogan 'Islam is in danger' and from here starts the cruel era of the exodus of Kashmiri Pandits. **"Raalib"**, **"Ghalib"**, and **"Chaalib"** sounds were echoing across the Kashmir Valley. The Kashmiri Pandits started targeting and were constantly threatened to leave the Kashmir Valley soon as possible via Urdu newspapers and even loudspeakers. After the appointment of **Jagmohan Malhotra** as the Governor Of Jammu and Kashmir on 19 January 1990, the targeting of Kashmiri Pandits increased. Several colonies and houses were burnt and Hindu women were raped! On this night, all the Kashmiri Pandits were forced to leave the Kashmir Valley. This night is called **"Quayamaat Ki Raat"**. This decade was the most painful decade for Kashmiri Pandits. They were shifted to the camps where also they were not at all safe. They started getting scared to even trust anyone. From this, we can understand their state of mind! Nearly 800 children became victims of stress and fear. Women also started getting complications in their body like early menopause even before the age of 35. Kashmiri Pandits tried to normalise their life. They started settling in Jammu, Punjab, Delhi and other parts of India. Is it so easy to forget this level of the deadliest past? Is it so easy to forget the years-old civilisation and adapt to the new climate and culture? Is it so easy to normalise life within a few days and Can we imagine that level of the incident? Never Ever. The shocking thing is that the world was completely silent! the **United Nations** also. Even their own country uttered a single word, neither from the opposition nor from the government!

The Kashmir issue is raised just for some political gains even today. Did these people get justice? Today also Kashmiri Pandits cry remembering their old past. Kashmir Matter is not only limited to territorial integration, it also meant cultural-civilisation integration. I won't quote any of the statements quoted in the past. But I only wish for Jammu and Kashmir's cultural civilisation and territorial integration.

Hurdles didn't stop there, they continued. Whenever a coalition government comes to power that too in the minority, internal disputes and ideological differences arise. The same happened with V.P Singh. Already there were 2 strong contenders- **Devilal and Chandrashekhar** for the Prime Miniter's post but V.P Singh got elected. Devilal wanted **Om Prakash Chautala** to be the Chief Minister Of Haryana, which he contested but due to the allegations of Booth Capturing and all, he was forced to resign as a chief minister. He contested again and became the chief minister again with the same previous techniques but this time Arun Nehru and some other leaders resigned, and BJP and Left Parties pressurized V.P Singh to take action against these activities. V.P. Singh resigned from his post but the party didn't accept the resignation. Devilal now was pressurized and finally, **Om Prakash Chautala** resigned as the Chief Minister Of Haryana. Devi Lal was sacked from the cabinet due to a fake letter regarding Bofors Scandal. The second issue faced was none other than **"The Mandal Commission"**. On 7 August 1990, the Government came up with the implementation of the Mandal Commission in the country and laid it on the table of the Lower House. This bill refers to 27% reservation for the Backward class. Morarji Desai set up this commission in 1989 to identify the backward classes of the society and to connect them to the mainstream under the chairmanship of **B.P Mandal,** Former Chief Minister Of Bihar. This report was submitted in the 1980s but was implemented in 1990. This bill faced many critics. Even the supporters of the government like Biju Pattnaik started criticizing the bill. The data collected by the **Mandal Commission** was based on 1930. This means that the bill was implemented just to create a political vote bank. Protests started against this bill. Many youths came onto the road and started protesting. The northern states of India were mostly affected due to the protests. BJP wanted the reservation on an economic basis, Rajiv Gandhi strongly condemned and said the way the British tried to divide based on caste and religion and today Raja Saheb is doing the same thing. We have taken the country to the edge of a caste war. Lathicharge, Teargases, etc. were used daily on the students. One of them performed self-immolation on the street during the protests near Police Headquarters in Delhi. Several cases throughout the country came after this incident. It was like

आगे कुवा पीछे खाई

like a situation for many political parties.

समर्थन किया तो upper caste नाराज और नहीं किया तो OBC नाराज

वोटबैंक भी तो बचाना है ना|

Finally, Supreme Court came into this matter and put a stay order on this implementation and things began to normalise. When **Lal Krishna Advani** was arrested in Samastipur during the **Ram Rath Yatra** carried out from Somnath to Ayodhya and Karsevaks reached the site on 30 October 1990, and by the orders of **Mulayam Singh Yadav**, police fired openly upon the Karsevaks. A deadly riot took place in Ayodhya on 2 November. BJP took back the support from the government and V.P Singh faced a no-confidence motion in parliament by 142-346 and he failed to prove the majority. Singh finally resigned on 7 November 1990. And after this, the phrase became popular in those days "**Mandal-Kamandal**". Supreme Court ordered for implementation of the Mandal Commission and ordered the removal of Creamy Layer to avail these facilities. In 2008, this was implemented also in the education sector also

After V.P. Singh's government collapsed, Chandra Shekhar took a chance, left the Janata Dal and formed Samajwadi Janata Party with **Devi Lal, Janeshwar Mishra, HD Deve Gowda, Maneka Gandhi, Ashoke Kumar Sen, Subodh Kant Sahay, Om Prakash Chautala, Hukam Singh, Chimanbhai Patel, Mulayam Singh Yadav, Yashwant Sinha, VC Shukla, and Sanjay Singh.** Rajiv Gandhi agreed to support Chandra Shekhar and on 10 November 1990, Chandra Shekhar was sworn in as the Prime Minister Of India. His government was largely seen as a "**puppet**" and "**lame duck**", and the government was formed with the fewest party MPs in the Lok Sabha. The 1991 Indian economic crisis and the assassination of Rajiv Gandhi plunged his government into crisis.

ᛈᛈᛈ

The complete detail of the Ayodhya dispute is in the next chapter

NINE

SAVIOUR OF INDIAN ECONOMY - SHRI. P.V NARASIMHA RAO

"In the high-profile political field, almost every important development could be traced to a clash of egos, sometimes necessary and beneficial, but often leading to catastrophe."

Since 1988, India has started moving towards the most significant economic crisis in times. Things became so worse that India had to pledge gold in 1991. All the dollar reserves were ended! Back times, the difference between the current account deficit and the fiscal deficit was so uneven that in 1988, **International Monetary Fund (IMF) Chief Michel Camdessus** came to India and discussed the situation with Rajiv Gandhi and said him that if this scenario continues, India will face a severe economic crisis in the upcoming days. But in 1989, Rajiv Gandhi lost the elections and V.P Singh became the Prime Minister Of India. V.P Singh's Government did nothing about this issue. Already the government was in minority and above all the Mandal Commission and protests, his government also collapsed within 11 months. The newly elected Chandra Shekhar Government came in 1990. Due to the Iraqi invasion of Kuwait, oil prices rose in International markets and so did India's expenditure per month. Chandra Shekhar's Government approached the IMF for a loan of 2 Billion Dollars. IMF put forth a simple condition that India has to allow the landing of Fighter Jets of the USA for refuelling purposes on their airbase. It's a phrase in Hind

मरता क्या न करता

Chandra Shekhar agreed to do so and US Fighter jets were refuelled on India's Airbase and IMF sanctioned the loan. But just getting loans to end this economic crisis in India? India has to mortgage its gold reserves to other countries like Switzerland, England, and Japan. Chandra Shekhar's Government collapsed. In 1991, India's fiscal deficit was close to 8.5% of the gross domestic product, the balance of payments deficit was huge and the current account deficit was close to 3.5%of India's GDP. India's foreign reserves barely amounted to US$1 billion, enough to pay for 2 weeks of imports.

P.V Narasimha Rao Ji

Pamulaparthi Venkata Narasimha Rao (P.V. Narasimha Rao Ji) became the Prime Minister of India on 21 June 1991. He invited **Dr Manmohan Singh**, the then-chairman of UGC to handle the Ministry Of Finance. RBI reduced the value of the rupee in front of the dollar. The IMF-dictated policy meant that the ubiquitous Licence Raj had to be dismantled, and India's attempt at a state-controlled economy had to end. There were no investments earlier, gradually Narasimha Rao Ji stressed public-private partnerships and liberalise the economy. Narasimha Rao Ji opened the doors for international investments. He united all the major opposition leaders and included them in his decisions. Markets started increasing at a speed because of the investments. Airline, telecom, TV broadcast and insurance were opened for private players. The consequences have been far-reaching. The opening up of foreign trade and investment boosted exports, services and inward remittances enormously. the post-crisis reforms of the early 1990s restored (then improved) the growth momentum of the 1980s and ensured a quarter century of nearly 6 per cent economic growth. With average living standards rising at almost 4 per cent a year, the poverty ratio dropped below a quarter of the population and the catchphrase of **"a rising middle class"** gained substance. Today, over 100 million Indians live in households with incomes between Rs 2 lakh and Rs 10 lakh a year. The strong improvement in the country's external finances and sustained growth over 25 years also raised India's economic and political profile in the world. In a real sense, the 1990s' economic liberalisation freed India's foreign and defence policies from economic weakness and dependence on foreign aid. A more assertive strategic policy became possible.

India was just getting out of the economic crisis, and at the same time a new scam came out **"The 1992 Indian Stock Market Scam"**. Recently in 2020, a web series is released on this topic, based on a book written by Mrs Sucheta Dalal. This scam was committed by Harshad Shantilal Mehta, a popular stock market broker and India's highest individual taxpayer of that time. He was also known as **"The Big Bull"**. In a ready-forward deal, securities were not moved back and forth in actuality. Instead, the borrower, i.e. the seller of securities, gave the buyer of the securities a BR. The BR serves as a receipt from the selling bank, and also promises that the buyer will receive the securities they have paid for at the end of the terms. Harshad Mehta was involved in defrauding SBI in which he took 1600 Crores from SBI and gave just 1100 Crores securities as per the records of RBI, which means 500 Crore was missing from the records. It was also found that NHB lend 500 Crores to Harshad Mehta. Many things came out. This turned out to be a scam which was exposed by a well-known talented journalist of The Times Of India, Mrs Sucheta Dalal. Harshad Mehta accused Prime Minister P.V Narasimha Rao Ji of corruption and said that he went to the PMO and gave 1 crore for the party fund in a press conference and his lawyer said that **"This is not Harshad Mehta Scam, it is P.V Narasimha Rao Scam"**.

Later on, a No Confidence Motion was carried out against the Government. The pressure was carried out on Rao to resign as the prime minister but he faced the motion. Most of the leaders and the parties were in favour of the No Confidence Motion and even people of his party were against him. But Finally, P.V Narasimha Rao played his master stroke and turned the game. He split 7 out of 20 MPs of **Ajit Singh**'s **JD(A)** and convinced 4 MPs of **Jharkhand Mukti Morcha (JMM)** to vote in his favour. Finally, his government survived this motion and he remained the Prime Minister though in the minority. There were allegations that Narasimha Rao gave money in exchange for votes which was later confessed by **Shailendra Mahto**, one of the MPs from JMM who vote in favour of P.V Narasimha Rao. After a CBI investigation, these allegations were found true but Supreme Court released them as the court denied considering Mahto's statement as proof. Strangely, many allegations were put against P.V Narasimha Rao during his tenure including the Purulia Arms Drop Case but none of them proved to be true. **अपना अपना नसीब हैं भैय्या.**

During the tenure of Narasimha Rao Ji, **Ayodhya Dispute** took momentum once again. It is said that the disputed structure was constructed by Mughal King Babar in 1528 on the place where Prabhu Shree Ram was born. Between 1528 and 1668, no text mentioned the presence of a mosque at the site. The Jesuit priest **Joseph Tieffenthaler,** who visited Awadh in 1766–1771, wrote, "Emperor Aurangzeb got the fortress called Ramcot demolished and got a Muslim temple, with triple domes, constructed at the same place. In 1885, Mahant Raghubardas Ji filed an appeal in **Faizabad District Court**. This appeal was cancelled saying that the structure was already constructed 325 years back so making a judgement, in this case, is not fair. On 21-22 December 1949 in the night, the idol of Prabhu Shri Ram appeared miraculously in the inner courtyard of the disputed structure. On 23 December 1949, FIR was filed in this case at the local Police Station of Faizabad. The place was sealed by the authorities. In 1950 **Gopal Singh Visharad** filed a title suit with the Allahabad High Court seeking an injunction to offer 'puja‘

at the disputed site. In 1986, Faizabad Court ordered the opening of the locks of the disputed site. and allowed Hindus to worship inside the "disputed structure". A Babri Mosque Action Committee was formed as Muslims protested the move to allow Hindu prayers at the site. The gates were opened less than an hour after the court decision. At that time Rajiv Gandhi was the Prime Minister of India. This decision was later criticized and questioned for the way of its implementation. The complete event was telecasted on Doordarshan TV. In 1989, during Kumbh Mela in Prayagraj, Hindu Organisations declare to keep the foundation stone of the temple in November. **Shila Pujan** started in many parts of India. All the Shilas were collected and were planned to send to Ayodhya. Many processions were carried out and VHP conducted talks with the Home Minister and Government gave the permission to perform Shilanyas in Ayodhya. Muslim groups protested against this ceremony. Riots started taking place in many places in India. Thousands of people lost their lives in Bhagalpur. Meanwhile, Rajiv Gandhi played a political stunt during election times by starting his political campaign from Ayodhya. He visited Ayodhya and declared to establish Ram Rajya back and appealed to vote for him in upcoming elections. Rajiv Gandhi lost the upcoming General Elections and V.P Singh became the Prime Minister of India. Lal Krishna Advani was arrested in Samastipur during the Ram Rath Yatra carried out from Somnath to Ayodhya. Karsevaks reached the site on 30 October 1990, and by the orders of Mulayam Singh Yadav, police fired openly upon the Karsevaks. A deadly riot took place in Ayodhya on 2 November. BJP took back the support from the government and the government collapsed. In the 1991 General Elections, P.V Narasimha Rao Ji became the Prime Minister of India. Meanwhile, BJP succeeded to win the mandate in the states like Himachal Pradesh, Uttar Pradesh, Rajasthan, and Madhya Pradesh. Kalyan Singh was sworn in as the chief minister of Uttar Pradesh at Ayodhya and gave the slogan-

राम लला हम आये है मंदिर यही बनाएँगे

Kalyan Singh seized the 2.77 Acres of the disputed site and gave it to **Ram Janmabhumi Nyas** on lease. Allahabad High Court put a stay on this decision and denied carrying out any kind of construction on the disputed site. Supreme Court asked UP Government to follow the instructions given by Allahabad High Court. Kalyan Singh denied indulging Central Police Force in this matter. On the appeal of Prime Minister P.V Narasimha Rao Ji, Karsewa stopped and was postponed till November. Talks started between Vishwa Hindu Parishad, **Babri Masjid Action Committee** and P.V Narasimha Rao Ji. Talks failed and VHP declared to resume Karsewa on 6 December 1992. Again on 8 November 1992, a meeting took place between both of them and that meeting failed. P.V Narasimha Rao planned to sack Kalyan Singh's Government but it also failed. The matter was going on in the court but the dates went on extending, 30 November, 4 December and so on. Finally, on 6 December 1992, symbolic Karsewa began marching towards the disputed site. Karsewaks started climbing the disputed structure and then started destroying the structure. 1-2-3 and the structure was destroyed. P.V Narasimha Rao tried to control the situation but nothing can be done now. Temporary Construction started for the temple. Kalyan Singh resigned after this incident and President Rule imposed on the state and this case continued in court. On 30 September 2010, The Allahabad High Court pronounces its verdict on four title suits relating to the Ayodhya dispute on 30 September 2010. Ayodhya land is to be divided into three parts. ⅓ goes to Ram Lalla represented by Hindu Maha Sabha, ⅓ to **Uttar Pradesh Sunni Central Waqf Board**, ⅓ goes to **Nirmohi Akhara. Akhil Bharatiya Hindu Mahasabha** and Uttar Pradesh Sunni Central Waqf Board moved to the Supreme Court of India, challenging part of the

Allahabad High Court's verdict. Supreme Court of India stayed the High Court order splitting the disputed site into three parts and said that the status quo will remain. On 9 November 2019, the Final judgment was delivered. The Supreme Court ordered the land to be handed over to a trust to build the Ram temple. It also ordered the government to give 5 acres of land inside Ayodhya city limits to the Uttar Pradesh Sunni Central Waqf Board to build a mosque. On 5 February 2020, The Government of India announced a trust to build a Ram temple there. It also allocated an alternative site in Dhannipur, Ayodhya to build a mosque to replace the demolished Babri Masjid. On 5 August 2020, Bhumipujan on the site was conducted by Hon'ble Prime Minister **Shri Narendra Modi** and the construction began.

Although Narasimha Rao Ji was the first Prime Minister who completed his term though being in a minority. He was also the first prime minister coming from South India.

Rao was the "true father" of India's nuclear programme.

Vajpayee Ji said that, in May 1996, "Rao told me that the bomb was ready. I only exploded it."

ppp

TEN

INSTABILITY IN INDIAN POLITICS

❦

"सत्ता का खेल तो चलेगा

सरकारें आएंगी जाएंगी, पार्टियाँ बनेंगी बिगड़ेंगी

मगर ये देश रहना चाहिए इसका लोकतंत्र अमर रहना चाहिए"

In 1996, P.V Narasimha Rao Ji's Government completed its term and elections were declared in India. The election delivered an unclear mandate and resulted in a hung parliament. Congress performed its lowest tally till now i.e. 140. BJP emerged as the single largest party in the house securing 161 seats.

After the announcements of the results, meetings started in the political corridors of Delhi. The Third Front started developing its political base, gathering all the parties and waiting for the right opportunity. V.P. Singh was the first choice for the third front. But V.P. Singh denied but Singh's first choice was **Jyoti Basu**, the then Chief Minister of West Bengal. But the central committee of CPI(M) declare that they will only support the government but won't participate in the cabinet. Jyoti Basu dropped as the Prime Minister candidate. Later on, after a few years, Jyoti Basu calls his party's decision a historic blunder. Jyoti Basu named **H.D. Deve Gowda(Haradanahalli Doddegowda Deve Gowda)** Ji as the Prime Minister of India.

Meanwhile, as per the protocol, **Shankar Dayal Sharma** invited **Atal Bihari Vajpayee Ji. Janata Dal, Samajwadi Party** and other parties protested against this decision. Finally, Atal Bihari Vajpayee Ji was sworn in as the Prime Minister of India. He was given time to prove the majority in the house. Samata Party led by **Nitish Kumar, Shiv Sena, Haryana Vikas Party and Shiromani Akali Dal** agreed to support the government but the number was just 194. To prove the majority, 272 votes are needed and it was not possible. It became clear that he did not have enough support to form a government. But BJP tried to convince other parties but this attempt also failed. Finally, Atalji resigned within 13 days after becoming the prime minister of India. This was the first time the Lok Sabha was telecasted live in the country. Atalji spoke brilliantly that day in the parliament. Here are some of the main points of the speech.

हम संख्याबल के सामने सर झुकाते है और आपको विश्वास दिलाते है की जो कार्य हमने अपने हाथ में लिया है वह जब तक राष्ट्र उद्देश्य पूरा नहीं कर लेते तब तक विश्राम से नहीं बैठेंगे

इस सदन में एक एक व्यक्ति की पार्टी... एकला चलो रे.... और चलो एक्ला अपने चुनाव क्षेत्र से और दिल्ली में आकर हो जाओ इक्कठे रे... किस लिए इक्कठे हो जाओ... देश के भले के लिए?... स्वागत है

हमारे प्रयासों के पीछे 40 साल की साधना है. ये कोई आकस्मिक जनादेश नहीं है. हमने म्हणत की है हम लोगो में गए है.. हमने संघर्ष किया है. पार्टी 365 दिन चलने वाली पार्टी है. ये कोई चुनाव में कुक्कुरमुत्ते की तरह से कड़ी होने वाली पार्टी नहीं है.

सदन को ठीक तरह से चलने में हम पूरा सहयोग करेंगे

मै अपना इस्तीफा राष्ट्रपति महोदय को देने जा रहा हु

Congress Party supported the United Front when **P.V. Narasimha Rao** was the President of the Congress Party. Disputes started within the Congress Party and Rao Ji had to resign as the President. Then, Sitaram Kesari took the position and removed Rao from the Parliamentary Committee. Sitaram Kesari wanted to have complete control of the congress party and the united front. It seemed that the complete system should work as per him. **Sitaram Kesari** started blackmailing the government on different issues. Finally, he took back his support from the government. It is said that Sitaram Kesari didn't consult the congress party about this matter. H.D. Deve Gowda while answering the debate in 1997, he said that the "**Old man was in a hurry to become the Prime Minister of India**". He is credited for providing financial closure and kickstarting the development of the **Delhi Metro Project**.

न खाता न बही, जो कहे केसरी वही सही

Inder Kumar Gujral

In 1998, Jain Commission reports leaked in the media. Many such facts came out. Various people and agencies are suspected of having been involved in the murder of Rajiv Gandhi. Chandraswami was suspected of involvement, including financing the assassination. The commission had inquired into the conspiracy aspects of the Rajiv Gandhi assassination. It reportedly criticised the **Dravida Munnetra Kazhagam (DMK)**, amongst others such as the Narasimha Rao government, for tacitly supporting Tamil militants accused in Gandhi's assassination. The DMK was part of the central ruling coalition and had ministers in the Union Cabinet. Congress threatened the government and asked Gujral to remove DMK from the cabinet or else, they will take their support back. Gujral want to handle the case legally but Congress took their support back.

Not only in **Jain Commission**, but Gujral also faced many internal disputes in the front in cases such as **"The Fodder Scam"** where the government forced the resignation of Lalu Prasad Yadav and other RJD ministers from the cabinet and **"Controversial President Rule in the state of Uttar Pradesh-1997"** where his government recommended president rule in Uttar Pradesh because Kalyan Singh passed the vote of confidence in Uttar Pradesh State Assembly. The Allahabad High Court also gave a decision against President's rule in Uttar Pradesh. He also resisted signing the **"Comprehensive Nuclear-Test-Ban Treaty"** to ban nuclear weapons test explosions and any other nuclear explosions, for both civilian and military purposes, in all environments which were adopted by **United Nations General Assembly**.

ELEVEN

AJATSHATRU IS BACK – SHRI. ATAL BIHARI VAJPAYEE

"भारत कोई भूमि का टुकड़ा नहीं है, यह जीता जागता राष्ट्रपुरुष है ।

ये वंदन की धरती है, ये अभिनन्दन की भूमि है ।

ये अर्पण की भूमि है ये तर्पण की भूमि है।

इसकी नदी-नदी हमारे लिए गंगा है, इसका कंकर-कंकर हमारे लिए शंकर है।

हम जिएंगे तो इस भारत के लिए और मरेंगे तो इस भारत के लिए,

और मरने के बाद भी गंगाजल में बहती हुई हमारी अस्थियों को कोई कान

लगाकर सुनेगा, तो एक ही आवाज आएगी-

"भारतमाता की जय"

श्री अटल बिहारी वाजपेयी

After the 1996 General Elections, BJP learned its lessons. They understood that it is not possible to win 272 alone. Already in 1996, BJP made their first impression 1996 in front of the country. But this was not enough. Though Atalji was made PM candidate for the upcoming elections, BJP understood that this is high time to improve their character. They have to shift towards central right ideologies from extreme right ideologies. Because the only reason why other parties didn't support BJP back in 1996 was their extreme communal ideologies. The experiments started in 1996 and BJP tried to unite other parties. This experiment worked for BJP and it was reflected in the 1999 General Elections. BJP won 182, Congres-141, and United Front-86. BJP finally established The **National Democratic Alliance (NDA)** in 1998. **Atal Bihari Vajpayee Ji** was elected as the leader of the NDA. Initially, **Shiv Sena, Samata Party, Akali Dal, and Haryana Vikas Party** allied with BJP. Later on **All India Anna Dravida Munnetra Kazhagam (AIADMK), Telegu Desam Party (TDP), Dravida Munnetra Kazhagam (DMK), Biju Janata Dal (BJD), All India Trinamool Congress (AITC), Lok Shakti, Paattali Makkal Katchi (PMK), Marumalarchi Dravida Munnetra Kazhagam (MDMK), Janata Party and TRC** allied with NDA. So on 19 March 1998, Vajpayee Ji was sworn in as the Prime Minister of India. **J. Jayalalitha** was the main pawn who collapsed the government. Vajpayee's government lasted 13 months until mid-1999 when the All India Anna Dravida Munnetra Kazhagam (AIADMK) under J. Jayalalithaa withdrew its support. It is said that Subramanyam Swamy played a very important role in the collapse of the government. The government lost the ensuing vote of confidence motion in the Lok Sabha by a single vote on 17 April 1999. See the dance of democracy. Just by a single vote! **"Each matters a lot in politics...."** The same AIADMK is one of the major alliances of the NDA and the same **Subramaniam Swamy** is a member of the BJP today. The government lost the ensuing vote of confidence motion in the Lok Sabha by a single vote on 17 April 1999. Sonia Gandhi, as leader of the opposition and the largest opposition party (Indian National Congress), was unable to form a coalition of parties large enough to secure a working majority in the Lok Sabha. Thus shortly after the no-confidence motion, President **K. R. Narayanan** dissolved the Parliament and called fresh elections. Atal Bihari Vajpayee remained the caretaker prime minister till the elections were held later that year.

During the 13-month term, Atalji took some very strong decisions of that time. One of them is **"Pokhran-II"**. The journey of making India a nuclear power started in 1948 after the formation of the **Tata Institute of Fundamental Research** and the entry of **Homi Jehangir Bhabha.** In 1954, Jawaharlal Nehru laid the foundation stone of the **Atomic Energy Establishment, Trombay**, known as **Bhabha Atomic Research Centre**. **Department Of Atomic Energy** was also established in India and Dr Bhabha was appointed as the secretary of the department. This department only reports to the Prime Minister. 1964, China conducted its first Nuclear Test at **Lop Nur** on **October 16, 1964**. It was a towering shot involving a fission device with a yield of 25 kilotons. Uranium 235 was used as nuclear fuel. China declared itself a nuclear nation. It was a threat to India as his neighbour cum enemy is now a nuclear nation. After Nehru passed away, Lal Bahadur Shastri came to power. Initially, Shastriji was not in favour of making nuclear weapons but later on, he was convinced. But in 1966, both Shastriji and Dr Bhabha passed away simultaneously. Indira Gandhi came to the power and on the other side, **Dr Vikram Sarabhai** became the secretary of the Department of Atomic Energy. When Indiraji realised the need for nuclear weapons in 1971, she cleared the programme in 1972. On 18 May 1974, Indira Gandhi conducted India's first successful nuclear bomb test. The complete operation was named **"Smiling Buddha"**. The Indian **Ministry of External Affairs (MEA)** characterised this test as a "**peaceful nuclear explosion**". Narasimha Rao Ji ordered them to be ready for the test anytime. In 1996, Vajpayee Ji started to test nuclear weapons but due to the minority votes, Vajpayee ordered to lower all the weapons. After then in 1998, Vajpayee Ji was ordered to be ready to conduct the test and after all discussions, 20 May was selected for the test. India successfully carried out. America was completely against India being a nuclear power. Strict monitoring was carried out by the USA through satellites and all the work had to be carried out at night only. This operation was named **"Operation Shakti"**. Code names were assigned to the scientists like "**Major General Prithviraj**" for **Dr APJ Abdul Kalam**, and "**Nataraj**" for **Dr R Chidambaram. Boom Boom Boom**- one after another- 5 detonations, the first of which was a fusion bomb while the remaining four were fission bombs.

"Today, at 15:45 hours, India conducted three underground nuclear tests in the Pokhran range. The tests conducted today were with a fission device, a low-yield device and a thermonuclear device. The measured yields are in line with expected values. Measurements have also confirmed that there was no release of radioactivity into the atmosphere. These contained explosions like the experiment conducted in May 1974. I warmly congratulate the scientists and engineers who have carried out these successful tests."

India immediately announced a no-first-use policy and is in the process of developing a nuclear doctrine based on "**credible minimum deterrence**". In August 1999, the Indian government released a draft of the doctrine which asserts that nuclear weapons are solely for deterrence and that India will pursue a policy of "**retaliation only**". The document also maintains that India "will not be the first to initiate a nuclear first strike, but will respond with punitive retaliation should deterrence fail" and that decisions to authorise the use of nuclear weapons would be made by the Prime Minister or his 'designated successor'. According to the NRDC, despite the escalation of tensions between India and Pakistan in 2001–2002, India remained committed to its nuclear no-first-use policy. In 1998, Bill Clinton, the then-President of the United States Of India said "**We are going to come down on those guys like a turn of brick**". Clinton imposed economic sanctions against India. In 1998 Pakistan also tested nuclear weapons and declared itself a nuclear power. Many countries across the world including the USA, China, Canada, Japan and many others countries stood up against India and criticized India on an international level. They also imposed economic sanctions against India. The USA and China even tried to make Kashmir Issue an international issue and tried to disturb the peace of both countries.

The main technical personnel involved in the operation were:
Project Chief Coordinators :

Dr A.P.J. Abdul Kalam (later, President of India), Scientific Adviser to the prime minister and Head of the DRDO.

Dr R. Chidambaram, Chairman of the Atomic Energy Commission and the Department of Atomic energy.

Defence Research & Development Organization (DRDO) :

Dr K. Santhanam; Director, Test Site Preparations.

Atomic Minerals Directorate for Exploration and Research :

Dr G. R. Dikshitulu; Senior Research Scientist B.S.O.I Group, Nuclear Materials Acquisition.

Bhabha Atomic Research Centre (BARC) :

Dr. Anil Kakodkar, Director of BARC.

Dr Satinder Kumar Sikka, Director; Thermonuclear Weapon Development.

Dr M. S. Ramakumar, Director of Nuclear Fuel and Automation Manufacturing Group; Director, Nuclear Component Manufacture.

Dr D.D. Sood, Director of Radiochemistry and Isotope Group; Director, Nuclear Materials Acquisition.

Dr S.K. Gupta, Solid State Physics and Spectroscopy Group; Director, Device Design & Assessment.

Dr G. Govindraj, Associate Director of Electronic and Instrumentation Group; Director, Field Instrumentation.

The situation started getting normalised between both countries. India and Pakistan both declared a new chapter of **Indo-Pakistan Cooperation** on 15 September 1998 in **New York**. In February 1999, Vajpayee travelled to Lahore through the bus service that started between both nations. Vajpayee Ji was welcomed with full honour. The resultant Lahore Declaration espoused a commitment to dialogue, expanded trade relations and mutual friendship and envisaged a goal of denuclearising South Asia. On the other side, Pakistani troops crossed the LOC and captured 132 vantage points controlled by India. Multiple infiltrations across the LoC are confirmed in Dras, Kaksar, and Mushkoh sectors. Vajpayee Government confirmed the news and decided to move out the Pakistani forces from Kargil. Though the government lost the confidence motion after Jayalalitha took back the support, Vajpayee Ji ordered the Air Force to take necessary actions but not to cross the Line Of Control. This operation was named "Operation Safed Sagar". **MIG-29** was under action and started destroying the Pakistani troops. As per the radio reports, 40% of the war essentials were destroyed by India. Direct involvement of the Pakistani army was proved and was declared by the Army Officials. India captured Tololing's peak. The Tololing peak is a dominant position overlooking the **Srinagar - Leh Highway (NH 1D)**, which is a vital link. The daily press briefing was done by Army Officials in Delhi. Even some journalists reached the site and covered the complete scene. **CaptainVikram Batra**, known as **"Shershah"** played a very important role in this war. Captain Vikram Batra comes from **Jammu and Kashmir Light Infantry**. His team captured Dras 0.4150 peak. Later on, 0.5140 was also captured by his team. But Shershah lost his life during the war. It was like-

> *"गड आला पण सिंह गेला"*

which means

> *"The fortress has come but the lion has gone"*

Today also, his one dialogue is very popular amongst the youth

> *Ye Dil Maange More......*

Nawaz Sharif tried to approach America and China but both of them denied it. Pakistani troops returned to Pakistan. Operation Vijay became successful.

After the Kargil War, fresh elections were announced in the country again. The BJP lead NDA won 303 seats out of 543. Atal Ji has been sworn in again as the country's Prime Minister for the third time.

Atalji faced the other challenge in 1999 when Indian Passenger aircraft was hijacked. In 1994, Masood Azhar was arrested in India from Anantnag when he was travelling to Srinagar on a fake identity card. He was imprisoned at the **Badami Bagh Cantonment** in Srinagar, **Tihar Jail** in Delhi, and lastly the Kot Balwal Jail in Jammu. Some attempts were made to blackmail the government into releasing Masood Azhar. The first attempt was carried out in 1995 when 6 foreign tourists were kidnapped in Jammu and Kashmir and demanded the release of **Masood Azhar**. One of them managed to run away and was found in August. The others were never seen or heard from since 1995. This attempt failed. The second attempt was carried out in 1999 when an Indian Passenger Crew was hijacked. In December 199, Indian Airlines Flight 814 was scheduled to fly between Kathmandu and Delhi. This Aircraft was hijacked by **Harkat-ul-Mujahideen(HuM)**. The Aircraft landed in Kandhar which was then controlled by the Taliban. HuM demanded to release 3 militants including Masood Azhar. Atalji had no option other than to agree to their demands. So finally Masood Azhar and 2 others were released by the Indian Government and all the passengers were brought safely back to India.

In upcoming times, India and USA relations strengthen, Vajpayeeji initiated talks with Pakistan, and invited Pakistani president Pervez Musharraf to Agra for a joint summit.

In 2001, Vajpayee Government again faced the terrorist. On 13 December 2001, some armed men with fake ID cards entered the Parliament Campus. The terrorists managed to kill several security guards, but the building was sealed off swiftly and security forces cornered and killed the men who were later proven to be Pakistan nationals. Vajpayee ordered Indian troops to mobilise for war, leading to an estimated 500,000 to 750,000 Indian soldiers positioned along the international border between India and Pakistan. Pakistan responded by mobilising its troops along the border. A terrorist attack on an army garrison in Kashmir in May 2002 further escalated the situation. As the threat of war between two nuclear-capable countries and the consequent possibility of a nuclear exchange loomed largely, international diplomatic mediation focused on defusing the situation. In October 2002, both India and Pakistan announced that they would withdraw their troops from the border. The Vajpayee administration brought in the Prevention of Terrorism Act in 2002. The act was aimed at curbing terrorist threats by strengthening the powers of government authorities to investigate and act against suspects.

Vajpayee's government introduced many domestic economic and infrastructural reforms, including encouraging the private sector and foreign investments, reducing governmental waste, encouraging research and development and privatising some government-owned corporations. Among Vajpayee's projects were the **National Highways Development Project** and **Pradhan Mantri Gram Sadak Yojana.** In 2001, the Vajpayee government launched the **Sarva Shiksha Abhiyan** campaign to improve the quality of education in primary and secondary schools. In late 2002 and 2003, the government pushed through economic reforms. The country's GDP growth exceeded 7% every year from 2003 to 2007, following three years of sub-5% growth. Increasing foreign investment, modernisation of public and industrial infrastructure, the creation of jobs, a rising high-tech and IT industry and urban modernisation and expansion improved the nation's international image. Good crop harvests and strong industrial expansion also helped the economy. In July 2003, Prime Minister Vajpayee visited China and met with various Chinese leaders. He recognised Tibet as a part of China, which was welcomed by the Chinese leadership, and which, in the following year, recognised Sikkim as part of India. China–India relations improved greatly in the following years.

One of the reasons why the BJP didn't retain power in 2004 is considered -the **"2002 Godhra Riots"**. On 27 February 2002, **19167 Sabarmati Express**, a train was coming from Ayodhya containing a Hindu pilgrimage. Approximately 69 passengers were burned alive in Coach No. 6. As per the verdict of the court, it is said that S5 and S6 were especially targeted by the mob. Second chain pulling was done when the train was passing through the entire Muslim area. Stone pelting and petrol were thrown from the on-side of the boogie. Some passengers tried to save their lives but many lost their lives. After this incident, VHP declared a **"Gujarat Bandh"**. Riots started in the state, especially Ahmedabad was the most affected city. Already in 2001, the state faced massive destruction due to the earthquake and in 2002, this incident took place. All the dead bodies were bought to Ahmedabad. Areas like **Naroda Patiya** were highly affected. Many people died in both communities and were affected a lot. Many local newspapers were criticised for increasing the tension in the state. Days after, the Gulbarg Society Massacre took place. The case went to court and many verdicts came till now. Vajpayee Ji also visited Godhra and Ahmedabad and met the victims of the riots. One phrase became very popular from that time-

चीफ मिनिस्टर के लिए मेरा 1 ही सन्देश है की वह **राजधर्म** का पालन करे

After this incident, **Ram Villas Paswan** resigned from the Cabinet Ministry. TDP demanded to remove Narendra Modi as the Chief Minister of Gujarat. Nitish Kumar applauded Narendra Modi. At that time, it is said that Vajpayee Ji wanted to resign from the post but **Jaswant Singh**, the then Finance Minister stopped him from doing so. On 12 April 2002, Narendra Modi described the Godhra Riots and laid his resignation on the table at the Goa National Meeting of BJP. Many parts of the hall were against the resignation of Modi. In the 2002 Gujarat Elections, Narendra Modi-led BJP won 127 seats out of 182 and Congress at 51. Narendra Modi's icon increased in the party and from here, Modi's journey starts. Modi's Vibrant journey will be discussed in the last chapter.

NDA was completely believed to return to power again in the 2004 General Election. Party came to the power in Chattisgarh, Rajasthan and Madhya Pradesh. Good Monsoon, Growth Rate @**8%**, Growing Economy, India Shinning Campaigning started in India. Most of the exit poll reports were in favour of the NDA government. It was pre-assumed that Vajpayee Ji will return to power again.***Bharat Uday*** and ***India Shinning*** campaigning carried out by BJP in India. But results were not at all in favour of NDA. Atalji said goodbye to politics due to his health issues. On 16 August 2018, at the age of 93, Vajpayee Ji passed away.

Once during his Lahore visit, a lady Pakistani press reporter asked him about his unmarried status. She said that she is ready to marry him on the condition if he gives her 'Kashmir' as a marriage gift. Without any hesitation, Atal ji replied, "Accepted, but only if you give me Pakistan as a dowry."

Numerous incidents in his life depict the vastness of his personality. He was a leader who was loved by people. He will remain in the hearts of millions.

Why "Ajatshatru"? - Vajpayee was referred to as the **Bhishma Pitamah** of Indian politics by former prime minister Manmohan Singh during a speech in the Rajya Sabha. "Atal Ji had an uncanny ability to connect with people from all walks of life and with political parties of different ideological moorings. Atal Ji had virtually no enemies.

ᐯᐯᐯ

सदवै अटल

मेरे प्रभु, मुझे इतनी ऊंचाई मत देना, गैरों को गले न लगा सकूँ, इतनी रुखाई कभी मत देना।

-श्री अटल बिहारी वाजपेयी

TWELVE

SINGH IS KING - DR MANMOHAN SINGH (2004-2014)

In 1997, **Sonia Gandhi** became the President of the **Indian National Congress.** Sonia Gandhi tried to revive the party but In 1999, Congress was reduced to 114 only. But in 2004, unexpectedly, Indian National Congress won the 2004 General Elections. At that time, Congress depicted Sonia Gandhi as the next Prime Minister of India. But the complete opposition denied accepting her as the next Prime Minister of India due to her foreign origin. Sonia Gandhi married Rajiv Gandhi in 1968 but she took Indian citizenship in 1983. This issue was also raised by many political parties in the 2004 General Elections campaigning. **Balasaheb Thackeray, Uma Bharti, Sushma Swaraj, Vajpayee Ji** and many others questioned her nationality and patriotism. Between 1997 and 2004, **Sharad Pawar** and **Mamata Banerjee** opposed her due to her Italian origin. Many of her supporters protested against her decision of resigning as the president of the Congress party. **Congress Working Committee**

expelled **Sharad Pawar, PA Sangma,** and **Tarik Anwar** for 6 years. All 3, later on, established a new party named Nationalist Congress Party. The same NCP is today one of the allies of the Congress-led UPA. BJP won 138 seats in the parliament and Congress 145. The complete UPA was at 218 and LEFT Front agreed to support UPA so the total was 277. NDA severely opposed Sonia Gandhi as the Prime Minister of India.

ये विदेशी पंत प्रधान हमें नहीं चाहिए

-बालासाहेब ठाकरे

Sonia Gandhi denied being the Prime Minister of India and many leaders as well as her supporters rigorously opposed her decision. Sonia Gandhi put forth the name of Dr Manmohan Singh as the Prime Minister of India. That's why he is called "**The Accidental Prime Miniter**".

The **National Advisory Council (NAC)** was set up on 4 June 2004 by prime minister Manmohan Singh, during the tenure of the first UPA government. Sonia Gandhi served as its chairperson for much of the tenure of the UPA government. As a chairperson of NAC, Sonia Gandhi was indirectly a cabinet minister. It seems that Prime Minister is Manmohan Singh but the powerhouse was NAC.

The NAC - II consisted of a mix of activists, bureaucrats, economists, politicians and industrialists-

Sonia Gandhi - Chairperson.

Mihir Shah - Member, Planning Commission.

Narendra Jadhav - former bureaucrat & Member, Planning Commission.

Ashis Mondal - Director of Action for Social Advancement (ASA), Bhopal.

Prof. Pramod Tandon - Vice Chancellor, North Eastern Hill University.

Deep Joshi - social activist.

Farah Naqvi - social activist.

Dr. N. C. Saxena - former bureaucrat.

Anu Aga - businessperson.

A. K. Shiva Kumar - economist.

Mirai Chatterjee - Coordinator, SEWA, Ahmedabad.

Isn't this seem like an alternative cabinet?

Apart from this, if we talk about the first tenure of Dr Manmohan Singh, he has tremendously contributed to the economy of India. Before 2004, India's Economy was growing @ **8**% and he maintained the rate even during the 2008 Global Financial Crisis. India was one of the least affected countries in the world. The GDP of India fell from 9% to 7.8% in 2008. India was the 2nd fastest growing economy in the world. Dr Singh's government introduced **MGNREGA** in 2005 to guarantee the 'right to work according to which rural areas were provided at least 100 days of wage employment in a financial year to at least one member of every household whose adult members volunteer to do unskilled manual work. NREGA was passed as an Indian Labour Law being implemented in 200 districts across India on 2nd February 2006. Later in April 2008, more districts were covered when the scheme was renamed to **Mahatma Gandhi National Rural Employment Guarantee Act (MGNREGA).**

One of India's biggest achievements under the government of Prime Minister Manmohan Singh was the signing of the **Indo-US Nuclear Deal** or the **India Civil Nuclear Agreement**. The framework for this agreement between India and the US was made in a joint statement by Manmohan Singh and the then President of the **United States of America, George W. Bush.** Under the agreement, India agreed to separate its civil and military nuclear facilities and that all civil nuclear facilities would be placed under the **International Atomic Energy Agency (IAEA).** The agreement was signed on 18th July 2005.

The **United States-India Peaceful Atomic Energy Cooperation Act of 2006**, or **Hyde Act**, is a US domestic law that modifies the requirements of Section 123 of the US Atomic Energy Act to permit nuclear cooperation with India, and in particular to negotiate a 123 Agreement to operationalise the 2005 Joint Statement. The US House of Representatives approved the bill on 28th September 2008. On 1st October 2008, the US Senate approved the civilian nuclear agreement allowing India to purchase nuclear fuel and technology from, and sell them to the United States.

One of the most significant achievements of Dr Singh is the **Right to Information Act (RTI)**. This act was passed to provide information on the work of every department. Every day on average, over 4800 RTI applications are filed. In the first ten years of the commencement of the act, over 17,500,000 applications had been filed. This notable legislation came under UPA in 2005 and has since then empowered every citizen of our country to ask for and get details of any publicly funded scheme, project or institution. It won't be wrong to say that this single piece of legislation has considerably changed India's governance realities.

The nuclear deal, RTI and MGNREGA were just a drop from the bucket, many other schemes were also launched like the **Nirmal Bharat Mission**, **SEZ Act**, the Launching of **AADHAR**, the Loan waiver for farmers, the Enactment of the Food Security Act and many more.

The 2009 Elections were fought in the face of Manmohan Singh Ji. Till then, Manmohan Ji and the UPA government were like a common man's government. BJP fought the elections in the face of Lal Krishna Advani Ji. Dr Singh didn't believe in taking credit for all the work done during his tenure. He just focuses on his work and that is unique about Dr Singh. He just believes talking is limited and short. Due to this quality, many others took advantage. Not only the opposition but also his party! During the election, **Lal Krishna Advani** attacked Dr Singh saying him the weakest Prime Minister till now. Manmohan Singh Ji won the 2009 General Elections and again became the Prime Minister of India for the second time. Surprisingly, Congress Party credited **Rahul Gandhi** for winning this election! The complete elections were fought on the face of

Dr Singh and his initiatives and works during his tenure and the victory credits are given to someone else, who just campaigned for UPA and that too for a few days!

Dr Manmohan Singh has sworn in again as the Prime Minister of this country on 22 May 2009. UPA got strengthened and won the Andhra Pradesh, Rajasthan, Maharashtra, Tamil Nadu, Kerala, West Bengal and Uttar Pradesh General Elections. India also won the ICC World Cup Champions Title under the captainship of Mahendra Singh Dhoni in 2011, after 28 years. But the second tenure of Dr Singh became one of the most controversial. Day by day, new scams were being exposed. **Coal scam: (2012), 2G spectrum scam: (2008), Chopper scam: (2012), Tatra truck scam: (2012), CWG scam: (2010), Cash-for-vote scam: (2011)**, **Adarsh scam: (2012), IPL scam: (2013), Satyam scam: (2009), Railway Scam** and many more. Is it so that Manmohan Singh was unaware of this all scams? Or someone was misusing the powers of Dr Singh as Prime Minister? During that time,**Kisan Baburao (Anna Hazare)**, a prominent social worker from Maharashtra raised his voice about the ongoing situation in the country and started "**Anna Andolan**". He demanded the appointment of **Jan Lokpal. Kiran Bedi, Arvind Kejriwal, Prashant Bhushan, Santosh Hegde, and Baba Ramdev** supported this Andolan. This Andolan got massive support from across the country. Anna went on to Incumbent Fasting. Andolan got momentum and lastly, the Government agreed. Jan Lokpal bill started to draft in the presence of civil society and the government of India but something failed. Meanwhile, Baba Ramdev declared "**Amaran Anshan**" against the corruption in the Ramlila Ground in Delhi. Talks between the Government of India and Baba Ramdev failed. The government took a lathi-charge on the protestors. Many people came to support Anna Hazare and this Anna Andolan got a huge public response throughout the country. The economy also declined in the second tenure of Manmohan Singh, Loksabha and Rajya Sabha were unable to function. Prime Minister remained completely silent in all the situations. Press Conferences were carried out by **P. Chidambaram** and **Kapil Sibal** to cover all the matters. Press Conferences were also conducted by BJP and continuously criticised. Eventually, Congress lost in Madhya Pradesh, Rajasthan and Chattisgarh state elections.

We talked about so many scams during Dr Manmohan Singh's tenure and also talked about terrorism and Andolans but answer my 1 question- Do you know about **"Operation Ginger"? I guarantee you that an 80% answer would be "NO". O**n 30 July 2011, during the tenure of Dr Singh, the Pakistan Border Action Team beheaded 2 Indian soldiers from Rajput and Kumaon Regiments, Hawaldar Jaipal Singh Adhikari and Lance Naik Devendra Singh in Kupwada. On 30 August 2011, Indian soldiers crossed LOC and beheaded 3 Pakistani soldiers and 8 were shot dead in response to the incident that took place on 20 July 2011. This Operation was conducted in just 45 minutes. **"Khoon Ke Badle Khoon Aur Sir Ke Badle Sir"** Dr Singh was misused because he never believes in propaganda, just his work. But many times, we forget even to admire the good steps of Dr Singh's tenure. I think so that's why Dr Singh once said *History will be kinder to me than the media.*

THIRTEEN

MODI MAGIC - SHRI. NARENDRA DAMODARDAS MODI (2014-PRESENT)

- 'अंधेरा छटेगा, सूरज निकलेगा, कमल खिलेगा'

-श्री अटल बिहारी वाजपेयी ,

"On the day of writing this chapter, (30/12/2022), PM Modi's mother Heeraba departed for Vaikunth Dham. There is nothing as priceless & indescribable in God's

creation as the bond between mother & child. I pay my heartly tributes to her and condolences to Honourable Prime Minister Shri Narendra Modi and his family. Om Shanti **"**

Between 2009-2014, new scams were exposed. Due to Anna Andolan, corruption news was known to everyone in this country. The Government which was once called a Common Man Government in 2009, the same government was called the "Government of Scams". Dr Manmohan Singh was called the "Remote Control Prime Minister". BJP also took complete advantage of the situation and attacked the government on the current situation in India. BJP lost the last elections of 2009. BJP was clear that this is the right time to change the leadership. BJP came up with **"Nayi Soch, Nayi Umeed"** and declared Narendra Modi as the Prime Ministerial candidate for the 2014 General Elections. With **"Nayi Soch, Nayi Umeed"** and **"Abki Baar Modi Sarkar"**, BJP campaigned for the 2014 General Elections and campaigned against corruption and price rise across the country. This campaign got momentum across the country. Modi showcased Gujarat Model in the campaigns and rigorously attacked Dr Singh and the ongoing government for corruption, price rise and silence of Prime Minister Dr Singh on the ongoing situation. In 2014, the BJP-led **National Democratic Alliance (NDA)** defeated its rival UPA with its highest number of seats. It was Congress Party's worst defeat in a general election with just 44 seats. NDA won 336 seats out of 543. BJP alone won 282 seats. It was a historic win for a ruling party after 1984. The third front just secured 77 seats. Narendra Modi was sworn in as the 14th Prime Minister of India and also the first prime minister born in independent India.

Modi Government took a positive approach to clean India. On 2nd October 2014, Modi launched the **"Swatch Bharat Mission"** to eliminate open defecation and improve solid waste management. the mission aimed to achieve an **"open-defecation-free"** (ODF) India by 2 October 2019, the 150th anniversary of the birth of **Mahatma**

Gandhi. The objectives of the mission's first phase also included eradication of manual scavenging, generating awareness and bringing about a behaviour change regarding sanitation practices, and augmentation of capacity at the local level. It is India's largest cleanliness drive, with three million government employees and students from all parts of India participating in 4,043 cities, towns, and rural communities.

Modi Government also took a positive approach to cleaning River Ganga by launching the "**Namami Gange**" programme to accomplish the twin objectives of effective abatement of pollution, conservation and rejuvenation of Ganga. It aimed at engaging with the UK community which will connect various interest groups including Scientists, Technology companies, Investors and community members. MCG(**National Mission For Clean Ganga**) has decided to declare ***Chacha Chaudhary*** the popular comic book character, as the mascot of the Namami Gange Programme a statement issued by the **Ministry of Jal Shakti**.

Modi Government initiated **Pradhan Mantri Jan Dhan Yojana**, a financial inclusion program that aims to expand affordable access to financial services such as bank accounts, remittances, credit, insurance and pensions. under this scheme, 15 million bank accounts were opened on the inauguration day. The **Guinness Book of World Records** recognized this achievement: "The most bank accounts opened in one week as a part of the financial inclusion campaign is 18,096,130 and was achieved by the Government of India from August 23 to 29, 2014".

Modi Government launched **Ayushman Bharat Yojana** which aims to provide free access to health insurance coverage for low-income earners in the country. Roughly, the bottom 50% of the country qualifies for this scheme. People using the program access their primary care services from a family doctor. When anyone needs additional care, then **PM-JAY** provides free secondary health care for those needing specialist treatment and tertiary health care for those requiring hospitalization. The programme is part of the Indian government's **National Health Policy** and is means-tested.

It was launched in September 2018 by the **Ministry of Health and Family Welfare**. That ministry later established the **National Health Authority** as an organization to administer the program. It is a centrally sponsored scheme jointly funded by the union government and the states. By offering services to 50 crore people it is the world's largest government-sponsored healthcare program.

Make in India is an initiative by the Government of India to create and encourage companies to develop, manufacture and assemble products made in India and incentivize dedicated investments into manufacturing. The policy approach was to create a conducive environment for investments, develop a modern and efficient infrastructure, and open up new sectors for foreign capital. The initiative targeted 25 economic sectors for job creation and skill enhancement, and aimed "**to transform India into a global design and manufacturing export hub.**"

"Make in India" had three stated objectives:

to increase the manufacturing sector's growth rate to 12-1 4% per annum;

to create 100 million additional manufacturing jobs in the economy by 2022;

to ensure that the manufacturing sector's contribution to GDP is increased to 25% by 2022 (later revised to 2025).

On 8 November 2016, the Government of India announced the **demonetisation** of all ?500 and ?1,000 banknotes of the Mahatma Gandhi Series. It also announced the issuance of new ?500 and ?2,000 banknotes in exchange for the demonetised banknotes. **Prime Minister Narendra Modi** claimed that the action would curtail the shadow economy, increase cashless transactions and reduce the use of illicit and counterfeit cash to fund illegal activity and terrorism. The announcement of demonetisation was followed by prolonged cash shortages in the weeks that followed, which created significant disruption throughout the economy. People seeking to exchange their banknotes had to stand in lengthy queues, and several deaths were linked to the rush to exchange cash. According to a 2018 report from the **Reserve Bank of Indi**a ?15.3

trillion of the ?15.41 trillion in demonetised bank notes, or approximately 99.3%, were deposited in banks, leading analysts to state that the effort had failed to remove black money from the economy. The **BSE SENSEX** and **NIFTY 50** stock indices fell over 6 per cent on the day after the announcement. The move reduced the country's industrial production and GDP growth rate. It is estimated that 1.5 million jobs were lost. The move also saw a significant increase in digital and cashless transactions throughout the country. Initially, the move received support from some central bankers as well as from some international commentators. The move was also criticised as poorly planned and unfair and was met with protests, litigation, and strikes against the government in several places across India. Debates also took place concerning the move in both houses of Parliament. In 2019, India experienced an economic slowdown which was attributed to demonetisation and several other factors. In 2020, a large number of users switched to digital payments with ease following the increase in the **COVID-19 pandemic in India**. The rise in digital payments and cashless transactions was attributed to demonetisation. Although with the new data released by RBI in Nov 2021, it is evident that cash circulation in India has increased multi-fold since demonetization and demonetization have not necessarily transferred cash users to digital users. As of November 2021, a further increase in digital payments and banknotes in circulation was seen.

On 1 July 2017, through the implementation of the 101 Amendment of the Constitution of India by the Indian government. which replaced existing multiple taxes levied by the central and state governments. **Goods and Services Tax (GST)** is an indirect tax (or consumption tax) used in India on the supply of goods and services. It is a comprehensive, multistage, destination-based tax: comprehensive because it has subsumed almost all the indirect taxes except a few state taxes. Multi-staged as it is, the GST is imposed at every step in the production process but is meant to be refunded to all parties in the various stages of production other than the final consumer and as a destination-based tax, it is collected from point of consumption and not point of origin like previous taxes. The tax rates, rules and regulations are governed by the **GST Council** which consists of the finance ministers of the central government and all the states. The GST is meant to replace a slew of indirect taxes with a federated tax and is therefore expected to reshape the country's $2.4 trillion economy, but its implementation has received criticism. Positive outcomes of the GST include the travel time in interstate movement, which dropped by 20%, because of disbanding of interstate check posts. Technicalities of GST implementation in India have been criticized by global financial institutions/industries, sections of Indian media and opposition political parties in India. **World Bank**'s 2018 version of India Development Update described India's version of GST as too complex, noticing various flaws compared to GST systems prevalent in other countries; most significantly, the second-highest tax rate among a sample of 115 countries at 28%.

GST's implementation in India has been further criticized by Indian businessmen for problems including tax refund delays and too much documentation and administrative effort needed. According to a partner at PwC India, when the first GST returns were filed in August 2017, the system crashed under the weight of filings. The opposition **Indian National Congress** has consistently been among the most vocal opponents of GST implementation in India with party President, Rahul Gandhi, slamming BJP for allegedly "destroying small businessmen and industries" in the country. He went on to pejoratively dub GST as **"Gabbar SinghTax"** after an ill-famed, fictional dacoit in Bollywood. Claiming the implementation of GST as a *"way of removing money from the pockets of the poor"*, Rahul has called it a "big failure" while declaring that if the Congress party is elected to power, it will implement a single slab GST instead of different slabs. In the run-up to the elections in various states of India, Rahul has intensified his **"Gabbar Singh"** criticisms of Modi's administration. According to an estimate, 230,000 small businesses shut down due to complications of compliance with the GST.

On 29 September 2016, India announced that it conducted surgical strikes against militant launch pads across the Line of Control in Pakistani-administered Kashmir, and inflicted "significant casualties". Pakistan rejected India's claim and instead claimed that Indian troops did not cross the Line of Control and had only skirmished with Pakistani troops at the border.

Indian media reported the casualty figures variously from 35 to 70. Pakistan accepted the deaths of two Pakistani soldiers and nine wounded. Pakistani sources reported that at least eight Indian soldiers were killed in the exchange, and one was captured. India confirmed that one of its soldiers was in Pakistani custody, but denied that it was linked to the incident or that any of its soldiers had been killed. Pakistan said India was hiding its casualties.

Media outlets noted that the details regarding the "attack" were still unclear. Earlier that month, four militants had attacked the Indian army at Uri on 18th September 2016 in the Indian state of Jammu and Kashmir and killed 19 soldiers. India's announcement of the claimed raid on 29 September marked the first time that the government had publicly acknowledged its forces crossing the Line of Control, amidst scepticism and disputing accounts. In the next days and months, India and Pakistan continued to exchange fires along the border in Kashmir, resulting in dozens of military and civilian casualties on both sides.

The Government formulated a bill and introduced it in the Parliament after 100 cases of instant triple talaq in the country since the Supreme Court judgement in August 2017. On 28 December 2017, the Lok Sabha passed **The Muslim Women (Protection of Rights on Marriage) Bill, 2017**. The bill was planned to make instant triple talaq in any form — spoken, in writing or by electronic means such as email, SMS and WhatsApp illegal and void, with up to three years in jail for the husband. MPs from RJD, AIMIM, BJD, AIADMK, and AIML opposed the bill, calling it arbitrary in nature and a faulty proposal, while Congress supported the Bill tabled in the Lok Sabha by law minister Ravi Shankar Prasad. 19 amendments were moved in the Lok Sabha but all were rejected.

As the triple talaq ordinance of 2018 was to expire on 22 January 2019, the government introduced a fresh bill in the Lok Sabha on 17 December 2018 to replace the ordinance.

The provisions of the bill are as follows:

- All declarations of instant triple talaq, including in written or electronic form, are to be void (i.e. not enforceable in law) and illegal.
- Instant triple talaq remains a cognisable offence with a maximum of three years imprisonment and a fine. The fine amount is decided by the magistrate.
- The offence will be cognisable only if information relating to the offence is given by the wife or her blood relative.
- The offence is non-bailable. But there is a provision that the Magistrate may grant bail to the accused. The bail may be granted only after hearing the wife and if the Magistrate is satisfied with reasonable grounds for granting bail.
- The wife is entitled to a subsistence allowance. The amount is decided by the magistrate.
- The wife is entitled to seek custody of her minor children from the marriage. The manner of custody will be determined by the Magistrate.
- The offence may be compounded (i.e. stop legal proceedings and settle the dispute) by the Magistrate upon the request of the woman (against whom talaq has been declared).
- The bill was passed by Lok Sabha on 27 December 2018. However, the bill remained stuck in the Rajya Sabha due to the opposition's demand to send it to a select committee

On February 26, 2019, in Balakot, a bombing raid was conducted by Indian warplanes in Pakistan against an alleged terrorist training camp. The airstrike was conducted by India in the early morning hours of 26 February when Indian warplanes crossed the de facto border in the disputed region of Kashmir and dropped bombs in the vicinity of the town of Balakot in **Khyber Pakhtunkhwa** province in Pakistan. Pakistan's military, the first to announce the airstrike in the morning of 26 February, described the Indian planes as dropping their payload in an uninhabited wooded hilltop area near Balakot. The following day on 27 February, in a tit-for-tat airstrike, Pakistan retaliated, causing an Indian warplane to be shot down and its pilot to be taken prisoner by the Pakistan military before being returned on 1 March. An **Indian Mi-17** helicopter was brought down by friendly fire in which all six airmen on board were killed; this was acknowledged by India on 4 October 2019. The airstrikes were the first time since the **India-Pakistan war of 1971** that warplanes of either country crossed the Line of Control and also since both states have become nuclear powers.

Several policies and programmes were introduced in India during 2014-2019 like "**Beti Bachao Beti Padhao**", "**Sansad Adarsh Sadak Yojana**", Merger of Indian Banks were also done during that time, Privatisation in many public sectors increased, Electrification of Railways, Constructing Highways @ 40km/day, "**Gati Shakti**", **Dedicated Freight Corridor, Atal Pension Yojana, Pradhan Mantri Ujjawala Yojana** and many more. The complete report card was collected and the 2019 General Elections were fought on all these issues. The plus point of this government was the clean image, free from corruption. There are many issues faced today also by the people, i.e. increasing price rise, declining of Rupee, and many more. In 2019, the BJP-led NDA won 353 seats of which BJP won 303 alone. The Congress-led UPA just 91 and Congress 53. BJP won with a massive margin and came back to power with Narendra Modi again as the Prime Minister of India. Moreover, the complete opposition was scattered, Congress Party was also scattered. There were internal conflicts between their allies and also in their party.

Today India has achieved a lot of things and a lot is left still! India has the potential to become the strongest country in the world. India has resources, talent, and leadership but only India needs to stop the brain drain. Why can't we give the same opportunity to those who left India? Some left the country for better opportunities and some left the country due to a lack of opportunity. Not only is brain drain an issue for India but the caste reservation is also the main issue why brilliant students are left behind. Moreover, the increasing population of India is also a major issue that India is facing today. Illiteracy is also a major issue in India but steps are taken very aggressively to eradicate it. But to achieve all, the government is not only responsible, but we also have to come forward and have to take the initiative. I have limited the journey till the 2019 General Elections. Thus I hereby conclude my book.

Thank You

Hope all the readers enjoyed the book.

Index

Chapter-5: Janata Sarkar- Shri. Morarji Desai (1977-1979)

Chapter-6: "Sweeping the polls"- Indira Gandhi Term III (1981-1984*)

Chapter 7: Youngest Prime Minister Of India"- Shri. Rajiv Gandhi (1984-1989)

Chapter 8: Raja Bahadur Shri. Vishwanath Pratap Singh (1989-1990)

Chapter 11: Ajatshatru is Back- Shri. Atal Bihari Vajpayee

Chapter 13: Modi Magic- Shri. Narendra Damodardas Modi (2014-present)

ᗞᗞᗞ

Bibiliography

Wikipedia: The Free Encyclopedia
Chapter 1: The Nehru Era (1952-1964)
1951–52 Indian general election. (2022, December 15). In Wikipedia. https://en.wikipedia.org/wiki/1951%E2%80%9352_Indian_general_election
Jawaharlal Nehru. (2023, January 2). In Wikipedia. https://en.wikipedia.org/wiki/Jawaharlal_Nehru
1957 Indian general election. (2022, August 29). In Wikipedia. https://en.wikipedia.org/wiki/1957_Indian_general_election
Chapter 2: "Man Of Peace" - Shri. Lal Bahadur Shastri (1964-1966)
Lal Bahadur Shastri. (2023, January 4). In Wikipedia. https://en.wikipedia.org/wiki/Lal_Bahadur_Shastri
Chapter 3: "Iron Lady" - Smt. Indira Gandhi (1966-1977)
Indira Gandhi. (2023, January 4). In Wikipedia. https://en.wikipedia.org/wiki/Indira_Gandhi
1967 Indian general election. (2022, November 17). In Wikipedia. https://en.wikipedia.org/wiki/1967_Indian_general_election
Chapter 4: The Dark Era of Democracy
The Emergency (India). (2022, December 20). In Wikipedia. https://en.wikipedia.org/wiki/The_Emergency_(India)
Chapter 5: "Janata Sarkar" - Shri. Morarji Desai
Shah Commission. (2022, June 16). In Wikipedia. https://en.wikipedia.org/wiki/Shah_Commission
Indira Gandhi. (2023, January 4). In Wikipedia. https://en.wikipedia.org/wiki/Indira_Gandhi
Chapter 8: "Raja Bahadur" - Shri. Vishwanath Pratap Singh
V. P. Singh. (2022, December 25). In Wikipedia. https://en.wikipedia.org/wiki/V._P._Singh
Chandra Shekhar. (2022, December 27). In Wikipedia. https://en.wikipedia.org/wiki/Chandra_Shekhar

Chapter 9: "Saviour Of Indian Economy" - Shri. P.V. Narasimha Rao

P. V. Narasimha Rao. (2022, December 30). In Wikipedia. https://en.wikipedia.org/wiki/P._V._Narasimha_Rao
Ayodhya dispute. (2022, November 4). In Wikipedia. https://en.wikipedia.org/wiki/Ayodhya_dispute

Chapter 11: "Ajatshatru Is Back"

Pokhran-II. (2022, December 20). In Wikipedia. https://en.wikipedia.org/wiki/Pokhran-II

Chapter 12: "Singh is King" - Dr Manmohan Singh

National Advisory Council (India). (2022, December 30). In Wikipedia. https://en.wikipedia.org/wiki/National_Advisory_Council_(India)
National Rural Employment Guarantee Act, 2005. (2022, December 17). In Wikipedia. https://en.wikipedia.org/wiki/National_Rural_Employment_Guarantee_Act,_2005
India–United States Civil Nuclear Agreement. (2022, October 23). In Wikipedia. https://en.wikipedia.org/wiki/India%E2%80%93United_States_Civil_Nuclear_Agreement
Right to Information Act, 2005. (2022, December 24). In Wikipedia. https://en.wikipedia.org/wiki/Right_to_Information_Act,_2005
Namami Gange Programme. (2022, December 13). In Wikipedia. https://en.wikipedia.org/wiki/Namami_Gange_Programme
Make in India. (2022, December 31). In Wikipedia. https://en.wikipedia.org/wiki/Make_in_India
2016 Indian banknote demonetisation. (2023, January 4). In Wikipedia. https://en.wikipedia.org/wiki/2016_Indian_banknote_demonetisation
Goods and Services Tax (India). (2022, December 7). In Wikipedia. https://en.wikipedia.org/wiki/Goods_and_Services_Tax_(India)
Triple talaq in India. (2023, January 2). In Wikipedia. https://en.wikipedia.org/wiki/Triple_talaq_in_India

2019 Balakot airstrike. (2022, October 31). In Wikipedia. https://en.wikipedia.org/wiki/2019_Balakot_airstrike
Pradhanmantri Series by ABP News
2013
LAL BAHADUR SHASTRI: Politics and Beyond
Publisher : Rupa Publications India (5 October 2019)
ISBN-10 : 9353336600
ISBN-13 : 978-9353336608
My Truth by Indira Gandhi
Publisher : Vision Books (15 February 2007)
ISBN-10 : 8170944686
ISBN-13 : 978-8170944683
Indira Gandhi: A Biography by Pupul Jayakar
Publisher : Penguin India (14 October 2000)
ISBN-10 : 0140114629
ISBN-13 : 978-0140114621
Indian Express (https://indianexpress.com/article/india/india-others/sunday-story-mandal-commission-report-25-years-later/)
Politics in India since Independence - TEXTBOOK IN POLITICAL SCIENCE FOR CLASS XII
Publisher : National Council of Education Research and Training; 2007th edition (1 January 2014)
Language : English
ISBN-10 : 8174507639
ISBN-13 : 978-8174507631
India After Independence 1947-2000 by BIPIN CHANDRA, MRIDULA MUKHERJEE, ADITYA MUKHERJEE
PublisherPenguin Books, 2000
ISBN0140278257, 9780140278255
Emergency Retold - Kuldip Nayar
Publisher : Konark Publishers Pvt.Ltd (30 November 2013)
ISBN-10 : 9789322008291
ISBN-13 : 978-9322008291
Last Days of the Morarji Raj by Barun Sengupta

Beyond the lines - Kuldip Nayar

Publisher : Lotus (1 January 2012)

Language : English

ISBN-10 : 8174369104

ISBN-13 : 978-8174369109

Memories of Gyani Zail Singh by Gyani Zail Singh

Publisher : Har Anand Publications; 1st edition (1 June 2002)

ISBN-10 : 8124105022

ISBN-13 : 978-8124105023

Ayodhya 6 December 1992 by Narasimha Rao

Publisher : Penguin (14 November 2019)

ISBN-10 : 0143442228

ISBN-13 : 978-0143442226

**Navabharat Times (https://navbharattimes.indiatimes.com/india/
history-of-declaration-of-emergency-in-the-country-on-june-25/
articleshow/83809257.cms)**

Rajiv Gandhi - The pragmatic Prime Minister by Satyavrat Ponkshe

Publisher: 1986 First edition, Bhate & Ponkshe, Pune.

My Country My Life by LK Advani

Publisher : Rupa (1 March 2008)

ISBN-10 : 9788129116543

ISBN-13 : 978-8129116543

The Scam - Sucheta Dalal and Debashish Basu

ISBN-10 : 8191013401

ISBN-13 : 978-8191013405

The Accidental Prime Minister by Sanjaya Baru

Publisher : Penguin Books Limited; 1st edition (11 April 2014); Viking

Language : English

Hardcover : 320 pages

ISBN-10 : 0670086746

ISBN-13 : 978-0670086740

Image Attributions

Dedication
Dr. (Er.) Alok Gupta, CC BY-SA 4.0
<https://creativecommons.org/licenses/by-sa/4.0>, via Wikimedia
Commons

Chapter 1
License: https://creativecommons.org/licenses/by/2.0/
Credit: https://www.flickr.com/photos/publicresourceorg/
26749023384

Chapter 2
By Unknown author - http://www.nehrumemorial.nic.in/en/
galleries/photo-gallery/category/
42-jawaharlal-nehru-with-other-indian-leaders.html, Public
Domain, https://commons.wikimedia.org/w/
index.php?curid=47028173

Chapter 3
Credit: https://www.flickr.com/photos/usembassynewdelhi/
11815578136
https://creativecommons.org/licenses/by-nd/2.0/

Chapter 5
Attribution: Photo division Government of India, Public
domain, via Wikimedia Commons
File URL: https://upload.wikimedia.org/wikipedia/commons/d/
d6/Morarji_Desai_portrait.jpg

Chapter 6
Prime Minister's Office (GODL-India), GODL-India
<https://data.gov.in/sites/default/files/
Gazette_Notification_OGDL.pdf>, via Wikimedia Commons

Chapter 7
By Government of India - https://www.invaluable.com/
auction-lot/
rajiv-gandhi-signed-6-x-4-b-w-portrait-photo-dated-129-c-0dd46e2b9d#,
Public Domain, https://commons.wikimedia.org/w/
index.php?curid=119118226

Chapter 8
Christian Lambiotte/EC, Attribution, via Wikimedia Commons

Chapter 9

Kandulareddy, CC BY-SA 4.0 <https://creativecommons.org/licenses/by-sa/4.0>, via Wikimedia Commons

Chapter 10

https://upload.wikimedia.org/wikipedia/commons/1/1b/Inder_Kumar_Gujral_071.jpg

Biswarup Ganguly, CC BY-SA 3.0 <https://creativecommons.org/licenses/by-sa/3.0>, via Wikimedia Commons

Chapter 11

Government of India, CC BY-SA 4.0 <https://creativecommons.org/licenses/by-sa/4.0>, via Wikimedia Commons

❧❧❧

Feedback

Please take the time and give your valuable feedback for this book. Please suggest to me the changes or content that should be added to this book. Don't hesitate to get in touch with patilaryan1504@gmail.com.

Please scan the QR code and provide your valuable feedback